SACF

O B J E C

D0460235

11/15

A book series about the hidden lives of ordinary things.

Series Editors:

Ian Bogost and Christopher Schaberg

Advisory Board:

Sara Ahmed, Jane Bennett, Johanna Drucker, Raiford Guins, Graham Harman, renée hoogland, Pam Houston, Eileen Joy, Douglas Kahn, Daniel Miller, Esther Milne, Timothy Morton, Nigel Thrift, Kathleen Stewart, Rob Walker, Michele White.

In association with

Georgia | **Center for**
Tech | **Media Studies**

BOOKS IN THE SERIES

hotel

JOANNA WALSH

Bloomsbury Academic
An imprint of Bloomsbury Publishing Inc

BLOOMSBURY

NEW YORK · LONDON · OXFORD · NEW DELHI · SYDNEY

Bloomsbury Academic
An imprint of Bloomsbury Publishing Inc

1385 Broadway
New York
NY 10018
USA

50 Bedford Square
London
WC1B 3DP
UK

www.bloomsbury.com

**BLOOMSBURY and the Diana logo are trademarks of
Bloomsbury Publishing Plc**

First published 2015

Library of Congress Cataloging-in-Publication Data
Walsh, Joanna.
Hotel/Joanna Walsh.
pages cm
Includes bibliographical references and index.
ISBN 978-1-62892-473-2 (pbk.:alk. paper) –
ISBN 978-1-62892-477-0 (ePDF) – ISBN 978-1-62892-476-3 (ePub)
1. Hotels–Miscellanea. 2. Hotels–Evaluation–Popular works.
3. Walsh, Joanna–Travel. I. Title.
TX911.2.W35 2015
657'.8374–dc23
2015008810

ISBN: PB: 978-1-6289-2473-2
ePub: 978-1-6289-2476-3
ePDF: 978-1-6289-2477-0

Series: Object Lessons

Typeset by Deanta Global Publishing Services, Chennai, India
Printed and bound in the United States of America

CONTENTS

PART ONE

HOTEL HAUNTING

1 HOTEL HAUNTING

"Nearly everyone hates hotels."
—GEORGE ORWELL, *DOWN AND OUT IN PARIS AND LONDON*

There was a time in my life when I lived in hotels.

Around this time, the time I did not spend in hotels was time I did not live. During this other time I haunted a marriage I was soon to leave. There's no place like home and, as home seemed hardly to qualify as a place any more, I began to look for something elsewhere.

I got myself a job as a hotel reviewer for a startup website. There was lots of reviewing to be done. I reviewed grand hotels and boutique hotels, budget hotels and expensive hotels, city hotels (mostly) and country hotels (occasionally). In each hotel I stayed one night, two, three at most. If I planned carefully, I could live in hotels for weeks at a time without taking a break.

What did I look for in hotels? A home away from home? Perhaps.

Some of the hotels I visited were like the homes I had sometimes thought I might have wanted as a child: baronial backstories of hunting prints and tartan (carpets, walls, bedcovers, everything!). Some were Zen gardens of mushroom minimalism; others, boudoirs, where terrifyingly tall satin bed heads and velvet button-back chairs Alice'd me into submission. Some hotels wanted to be better than home: seamless, uplit concept spaces; entire rooms dipped in white rubber (a few scuff marks around the feet of the bed); corridors with no lights; walls that changed color at the flick of a switch; black toilet paper.

A few hotels, wishing to be more homelike, installed nervous "lounges," and "libraries" in their lobbies; these usually contained a very few books, artfully arranged, their covers glaring from dark recesses. The books were art books mostly, and mainly photographic—landscapes, travel, architecture—books about places as far from the hotel as the hotel was from home. As inoffensive and impersonal as the artificially aged leather chairs into which I sank with a kind of pre-made comfort, they were nothing I could settle into. Some of these "lounges" and "libraries" had "honesty" bars which, by their very name, provoked temptation. Several of them displayed cakes and biscuits as well as bottles, but could I take the last slice or be discovered in this very public privacy, covered in crumbs? Set too near to the hotels' revolving doors, they were chilly places and largely unfrequented, as were the hotel restaurants, except at breakfast, which was sometimes included in the deal, and sometimes not.

My first hotel was both grand and boutique: a new hotel in a three-centuries-old townhouse in a walled garden in the middle of a city. Its Unique Selling Point was privacy, but the owners wanted a review all the same.

The French-born manager met me in the garden. She apologized, "The designer did not want flowers. Flowers are a little . . . vulgar. We wanted the garden to be like the hotel. There are lots of places where you can be private. That's why we don't have a name on the door. You have to find the hotel. It's like a secret."

It *had* taken me a little time to find the hotel, dragging my wheeled suitcase up a cobbled hill in the August heat. The price of rooms ensured that any paying guests would arrive by taxi.

We pushed through plate glass doors into the lobby. It was beautiful: each surface polished, reflective, dazzling. There was marble, there were mirrors and, inside *vitrines* around the shining walls, there were goods for sale: face creams, commemorative trinkets, cultured pearl earrings, all with discreet price tags; in one *vitrine*, the crumbling eighteenth-century bill of sale for the hotel building sandwiched between two pieces of glass. Sitting in the rear formation of the lobby's three groups of tastefully mismatched retro-modern and antique gilt chairs, a fat man took phone calls. Pugnacious and balding with a small, square beard, he looked like he might have been the hotel's catering supplier, or a visiting movie director. He wore a loud, striped shirt. His leather jacket may have been exquisitely distressed by design or bought from a local street market. He looked as though he could be very rich. Rich enough not to care.

The desk clerk handed me a key. I left my luggage and checked into hotel terminology, which is all tautology and bad puns (I once glimpsed the *Terminal Hotel* through a train window at Milan station). Hotel lingo is parallel to everyday speech for, on vacation, who acts exactly as they do at home? It moves on restlessly to the last resort, coupling ill-matched lexical strangers in "lounge-bars," "activity-holidays," "hospitality-suites," though some of its cocktails—"pillow-menu," "mini-bar"—can be hard to swallow.

Hotel was once a word for house, but at some point the term took a turn. Now "Hotel" stands for "difference," which is sometimes inversion (why say, "splendid hotel," when you can declare, "Hotel Splendid"?) and sometimes appropriation (say, "maitre d," "patio," "tapas," not, "waiter," "yard," "snacks"). Restless as their vocabulary, hotels across the world are named for elsewhere, each displaced by a city or two: the Hotel Bristol in Paris, the Hotel London in New York and, in Berlin, the Hotel de Rome—not to mention the Orientals, the Swissotels, the InterContinentals that pinpoint the globe.

Is a hotel a language system? It's a system of some kind: a series of set elements in different combinations. All hotels invite decoding and every hotel is a "concept hotel." I love to read about hotels I have never seen or stayed in, hotels that once stood for something to a reader at one remove in place or time. Joan Didion's hotel writing induces the ecstatic vertigo of an entirely self-referential lexicon. Hotel Barbizon, fictionalized by Sylvia Plath in *The Bell Jar* as Hotel Amazon, is a double signifier for which I have no referent. Names to conjure with! Who cares if these hotels exist and, if they do, whether I will ever visit? The glamour of the entirely unknown is the ultimate in name-dropping.

Many of the hotels I reviewed had recently reinvented themselves but, reopening, seldom thought to change their names; perhaps there is a finite number. "There is a *Grand Hotel* in every city," says Lionel Barrymore in Edmund Goulding's 1932 film that, as if to illustrate his point, is also called "Grand Hotel." In the days of Goulding's movie, purpose-built hotels were the last word in chic and new structures required newly invented names: Starwood (founded 1930), Novotel (1965), Accor (1967). Nowadays, rather than neologize, hotels re-purpose. There are hotels in caves, in trees, on rivers, in the ice, in anyplace that's no place like home. I've stayed in hotels that were once palaces, car parks, brothels. They do not so much wish to leave their original occupations as revisit them in fantasy terms, as ghosts of their former selves. The old "new" hotels used to pride themselves that every room was the same; the new "old" hotels boast that every room is different. Chain hotels bind us to the expected ("Recollection's love," concluded Kierkegaard, checking into a Berlin guesthouse that disappointed on a second visit, "is the only happy love.")[1] but boutique hotels make a virtue of the local, each of them influenced by its particular place in the world. In these hotels, rooms are named, not numbered.

It feels personal, but it's not *your* personal. You adapt yourself to the room's desires, and it promises to return you to the non-hotel world fitter, chic-er, hipper than on your arrival.

In Paris there is even a Hotel de l'Avenir (Hotel Future), which I have never visited.

"I treat hotels, even sleazy specimens," says poet and cultural critic, Wayne Koestenbaum, in his book, *Hotel Theory*, "as utopias." How *do* hoteliers do it? I wonder. Or, rather, why? Who'd take up the profession without boundless optimism, boundless generosity, boundless cynicism about the nature of human desire? I'm here to try on someone else's version, not of my life, but of an ideal life, cut to my budget. Like the towelling robe in the bathroom, it feels good but it doesn't really fit. Nevertheless I'll put it on. I insert my keycard into the slot. The handle turns. I'm in.

They're keen on black here. And white. The floor of my room is slate. A huge pale bed rises from it on a central platform. I stumble like a pilgrim as I approach, missing a step in the dark gulf of the floor. I pick myself up. My bed must be six feet square, seven. Goldilocks, I spread myself across it to check. It is wider than I am tall.

Now I am in, what do I do? I had envisaged my hotel-self working all afternoon, my bed strewn with books and papers but, somehow, I can't get started. However much they try to shake it up, provide "experiences," hotel terminology exists to soothe and relax. Staff pillow conversations with long, formal sentences. Not "No Problem," advises Doug Kennedy, provider of training programs for "guest service excellence" and "front desk profit optimization," but "It was my pleasure." Or "You are most welcome." Hotels—hushed—have a problem with the active voice. The passive evades clock time and diffuses responsibility (not "We're serving your dinner at eight," but "Dinner is served."). To *stay* in a hotel is never like *living* at home. Hotel is a nothing-doing, but hardly through what I would call choice. Like Miss Golightly, I am "travelling." Nevertheless I have—simultaneously—arrived.

What *should* I do in a hotel room? I look around for clues. Some of the things in my hotel room, pretty as they are, are merely for use and, as such, uninspiring. Others, being purely decorative, are puzzles without solutions. The eternal hotel-room question is *what am I allowed?* Should I pull the curtains—is there a cord? How do I control the air-conditioning? What is the WiFi password? Can I open this window? I put out a hand to stroke the gilt serpent, hand-stencilled by a well-known graphic artist, that snakes across the wall. It is scaly with crackled lacquer. Electric buttons are hidden in the wallpaper. I push one and, leaning toward the head of the snake, I hear a faint hiss. As I turn away a useless vase of purple liquid, poised on a small tray-table, overbalances and crinkles, almost mutely, into cartoon diamonds on the carpet. Did I do something wrong? Hotel bedrooms are invitations to failure. In my time I have accepted many of these, eventually concluding that I am unlikely to survive a hotel visit without breaking something. Then there are the personal tripwires: How much should I tip? When should I call room service? As someone trained to ask for little, to make as little fuss as possible, I am in truth badly suited to my job. In order to become a guest I must learn to adjust the horizons of my desires.

A knock at the door. It's the manager with something complimentary.

"You like the room?"

"It's . . . fantastic."

"You would like me to show the bathroom? It is very Philippe Starck influence. Influence—is that a good word?"

"Yes."

In a city where most apartments have space for no more than a shower cubicle, my en-suite has a bath. As white, almost as big, as my bed, any bather is no more than a specimen on a marble slab. I notice the egg-shaped toilet, wall-mounted slightly too high, like the bed. There is the black toilet paper waiting beside its white alternative and, on the shelf, a "babapapa nostress": a squeezy toy you can press to relax, around it a band of cellophane that tells me it's not included in the deal.

"We are a boutique hotel," the manager explains, "so we have various items available."

I'd been under the impression that "boutique" referred to the size of the place and its independent style, not to the fact it sold things.

She indicates a menu by the bed. The hotel offers other overpriced toys: "erotic" chocolates, jelly-flavored condoms. As well as the "nostress," you can buy incense and "calming" bubble bath. The hotel sells you misbehavior, then something to deal with the fallout, both in candy colors. There's a pointed notice in the bathroom: "If you would like to take away a souvenir, our robes are for sale at reception." The hotel mistrusts me. I'm not surprised. There's no right or wrong here. Despite the bedside drawer's insistent Bible, the usual moral standards do not apply. This is my holiday, my treat. I've come for what I'm owed, and more. The disappointments of my life may revenge themselves in petty larceny, but, even then, will I get what I've paid for?

How am I in a hotel? Although enraged, I whisper. But I will enthuse when required. I will delight in what is put in front of me, unsure I would delight in such a thing at home. *A tour of the hotel? For my review? I'd love to.* I follow the manager. Shame works its way under our skins as she unlocks door after door, as we cross thresholds to find guests' clothing unpacked, underwear straddling the chair backs, surprised electricians balancing on sinks to repair light fittings, cleaners removing bin-loads of empty bottles. More shameful yet (in a world where the guest must appreciate the value of everything and the price of nothing) are the workings of the hotel's mind laid bare. "This is our most expensive room," my guide is forced to admit. "This room is designed to appeal to ladies, this to economically-inclined families . . . . This room is 'specially equipped for romance.'"

"We didn't want to be like the big hotels," the French-accented hotel manager tells me. "We have only seven suites. In this space, we could have had fifteen. Big hotels are sometimes a bit . . . impersonal. We wanted to do something more personal. We want the ghosts (she modulates the vowel in 'guests') to feel at home . . . not like in a ghosthouse. But the hotel is also not somebody's home. We want ghosts to be left alone—or to have conversations with other ghosts if they want to."

Desire, being not so easy to fool, however, feels a disjunction between itself and what arrives to answer it. In that gap, disgust grows like mold between tiles. Intimacy was something I'd come to escape; didn't she understand? But I cannot avoid the ghosts.

Like Greta Garbo in Edmund Goulding's 1932 movie, *Grand Hotel*, I wanted to be alone, but in truth I was never left alone. It was not my fellow guests who, like me, seemed to have come here to get away. Other ghosts with passkeys stole into my room unannounced, if I did not bar them by hanging a totem of cardboard on silk rope around my door handle. They left small tokens of their presence: a newspaper, the corner of a sheet turned down; a single melting chocolate on my pillow; toilet paper folded into a v—sometimes no more than that. In the corridors they hardly disguised themselves. It was strange how—once outside my door— they were willing to be seen in the flesh, their tiny treasures spilling from tall steel shelf-stacker trollies. Inside my room they dissolved into a mist of might-have-been, but I always met one pushing through the lobby in the morning, in the way of breakfast.

A ghost erases the present by repeating the actions of the past. That's what haunting is. Was this what I wanted from hotels—to be haunted? Was it the gleaming tiled bathrooms I hadn't cleaned, was it the beds I hadn't made, that magically remade themselves every time I left the room, my own presence constantly smoothed over? Was it the clean sheets that had nevertheless been slept in by so many others: old and young, sick and well, couples and singles? Was it the clinical paper that put itself between me and the room's objects: the "police—do not cross" strip across the toilet, the miniature soaps wrapped with no more than one end-user in mind?

But hotels are never successfully haunted. Hotel ghosts might go through the motions but it's homes (usually stately) that are haunted, by ghosts that are in the family, or at least familiar. A ghost is an exegesis—it comes to point the finger, tell the true story—but hotels like to make up their own histories in keeping with the fashion, remake them each time they make up your room.

A hotel, restless, cannot be a home, not even a home away from home; far from it. It puts the mockers on home and all that is homely. A ghost must be seen by the living in order to exist (if we are all dead, a ghost is nothing but a neighbor); a hotel sets itself apart from home and, in doing so, proves rather than denies home's existence.

Sigmund Freud in his 1919 essay, "The Uncanny," tells how the word *heimlich* ranges in meaning from "homely" to "private"and from "private" to "secret," and thence to "dishonest" and on to "uncanny," and that *unheimlich*, home's apparent opposite, stands for no more than the uncanny inner workings of the homely, uncovered.

A hotel's secret is that it's only a seeming mini-break from the rights and wrongs of home. A hotel is an occasion for *unheimlich* longing. That so few hotels are satisfactory may be part of the trick. We expect our desires to be addressed and dispensed with. Instead, they are put on ice. We're numbed. So what: *What-isn't* can be richer, more ornamental, than *what-is*. But, in constructing a hotel, you can't keep out the human element. A hotel's glamour is its guests. We must live up to our hotels. We're on display; we're what's being sold. No need to ask us in like vampires: we invite ourselves. We are paying ghosts.

I return, with the hotel manager, to my room, to find the broken vase spirited away without mention, end of story. My mistakes do not come back to haunt me. Instead, I must learn how not to fear the consequences.

* * *

Going down to breakfast the next morning I comply a little with my surroundings, put on lipstick. As I enter the lobby I am aware of the looks, the smiles, some of which have been paid for, but not by me. As a reviewer I am only performing being in a hotel, after all. The hotel might be footing my bill, but it won't let me get away with nothing in exchange. As I'm not a consumer, it will gobble me up through the words I will write. I am but a tiny organ of the system with no immediately obvious function: a hotel appendix.

I find the dining room closed. On its terrace a group of women from a fashion magazine shoot a model in a floral trouser suit against the lush wall of blossomless chic bamboo. They have hung expensive dresses on cheap wire coat hangers in the expensive door frames. I have to duck under them to pass. Why did they choose this hotel?

A hip hotel is a palace on an edgy street, or a ghetto in a bourgeois neighborhood. Like fashion, what *makes* it is always its difference, as required as the loneliness we slip on as we cross a hotel threshold. The fashion women sit at a garden table in a mess of colored pots of eye shadow, ashtrays, discarded hats and shoes. Like me they are dressed informally: jeans, Converse, army surplus jackets. They are familiar with luxury; intimately connected. They promote it, sell it, but they do not participate in it.

Forgetting breakfast, I wheel my case down to the lobby, preparing to haul it back down the cobbled hill to the Metro and my next hotel. There's no rest for the wicked.

As soon as you're in a hotel, you'll want to get out—at least that's what the receptionist behind the desk is there to tell me, proffering a sheaf of maps and discount entry offers. I catch myself longing for the cheap trashiness of the real. In the street outside the hotel I know there are stalls selling "I heart" T-shirts and snow globes enclosing the city's monuments. I know there is bad takeaway coffee and that there are queues of tourists happy to drink it. I check out.

As I wait for my receipt, I flick through telephone-directory-thick architectural magazines. The fat bearded man still haunts the square of chairs, or he is there again. *Is* he rich? Like many rich people, he seems mildly but constantly irritated. I notice a notice by the front door. The designer chairs in the lobby are only temporary. They are for sale. As is the art on the walls.

The rich, fat man takes delivery of a Japanese takeaway. He returns to his table in the corner and unpacks two large trays of gleaming pink sushi, three of glutinous, translucent rice, two closed brown paper bags and a cardboard noodle box. It is all for him. He has everything he could wish for, more. In the privacy of the secret hotel, he arranges his trays on the low table before him and, bending uncomfortably at the waist, reaches for his chopsticks and begins to eat through them, one by one, with dogged, unpleasured stolidity. The delivery guy waits for a tip. Then fades. He doesn't get one.

The Belgian philosopher Raoul Vaneigem feared such encounters.

"Remarks, gestures, glances tangle and collide, miss their aim, ricochet like bullets fired at random, killing even more surely by the continuous nervous tension they produce. All we can do is enclose ourselves in embarrassing parentheses; like these fingers (I am writing this on a cafe terrace) which slide the tip across the table and the fingers of the waiter which pick it up, while the faces of the two men involved, as if anxious to conceal the infamy which they have consented to, assume an expression of utter indifference."

But perhaps that was what I wanted from hotels: the impersonal; the comfort of strangers. Orderly ways to be. The same big joyful con as in the movies where everyone knows that the performers, like dinner-jacketed waiters, will leave through the service entrance in jeans to climb onto their mopeds or slouch off to the metro. Hotels are for those who understand performance: ghosts, actors, women . . . . To hold onto its clientele a hotel must understand performance well enough to create a certain amount of traction.

Still, there's no place like home, and the hotels knew it. As if in apology for this deficiency, when I arrived at my hotels I was offered whole hospitals of fruit baskets and flowers. I was offered bottles of wine and sometimes, if I was lucky, champagne. I was offered chocolate lollipops, boxes of pastel macaroons (these things never happened at home!). I was offered, once, oddly, a hook on which to hang my bag beneath the breakfast table, stamped with the hotel's enameled crest. It was decorative, but also suggested that during my stay I should be wary of loss.

There was always something, the hotels suggested, that I should worry about losing.

What did I gain? I was not paid for my hotel reviews, but neither did I pay for the promise of escape they provided. Along with escape, I was offered the prospect of return. These hotels wanted me for life. When I left, one gave me a tiny tinkling golden charm to hang around my neck—the hotel's logo. One gave me a key ring, another a potted candle, each embossed with the hotel's gilt initials. Would I return? It being my job to review many different hotels, almost none of which I could normally afford even on special occasions, I never did.

By the end of one month during which I'd lived in hotels almost all the time, I got sick. Inside the white stone walls of my last hotel—a medieval convent whose rooms were of the mushroom-colored, Zen type—the bath would not run hot. No longer able to tell whether this was my fault or someone else's, no longer having the energy to call room service to get it fixed, I took a chill, and went home to a place where what was expected of me was less formalized, if more rigorous. There, if anyone gave me anything, something would be expected in exchange, though there was never any tariff fixed to the back of the bedroom door, along with instructions for escape.

PART TWO

FRAGMENTS FROM A HYSTERICAL SUITCASE

2 HOTEL FREUD

```
Cast:
Freud:              a psychoanalyst
Dora:               a teenage girl
Mae West:           a sex symbol
Groucho Marx:       a member
A Friend:           a friend
```

I

Dora, a teenage girl, lives at home with her mother and father. Her father is a factory owner; her mother is a homemaker. Her mother has a household disease—a disease in which she makes too much home, too much for the people in it, so much that it makes them want to leave.

Dora's father "was often absent, visiting his factories," and, "In high summer he went to a spa in the mountains," for "his pulmonary complaint." On these trips he stayed, where? In a hotel, in a clinic? Not feeling at home, Dora (her father reports) "*insists*" that she will join him at the spa.

Dora goes, with her dad, to the spa. They stay where they are not at home. *Unheimlich* things (involving family, familiarity) happen there nonetheless.

By the lake at the spa resort, a man tries to kiss her; older, her father's friend, her father's lover's husband. She is eighteen.

Aphonia—Dora began to say nothing. Like her aunt, who didn't eat, and died "after an unhappy married life," she shut herself up: nil by mouth.

Dora's father took her to see Dr. Freud.

She had been reading, at the time, her father reported, a book about sex. Perhaps she imagined the whole thing.

Perhaps words manifest off the page.

Silent Dora consented to talk to Freud.

Freud said, as she was kissed, Dora had felt "not only the kiss on her lips but the pushing of the erect member against her body. . . . And the stimulation of that second erogenous zone has been fixated by displacement on to the simultaneous sensation of pressure on the thorax." She found this so unspeakable that she became silent.

Freud wanted to reveal the truth, the *unheimlich*, which is, he said in his essay, "The Uncanny," contained within the *heimlich* (or is it the other way round?). He thought the truth was something that had to be revealed, and that you could do this with words, and Dora's case was the first he made into a story by writing it down. Freud chose to believe Dora, not her dad, but Freud thought there was something wrong with Dora's words. He thought that, though she didn't complain, she had a complaint that could be cured by new words, by a talking cure.

A disease of language, then?

II

FREUD
She always spoke very dismissively
of doctors, whom she had evidently
overrated in the past.

I check into home. I have been in a hotel. There is no one at home. It feels like there has been no one there for some time. The lights are off; some of the curtains are closed. Some things have been left around. I can feel the presence of your absence.

I don't like the way everything is at home here, the unhomely inside the homely. Home contains everything, after all; even its opposite, Hotel. Does home contain workplace, library, office, conference room, all those places outside home, from which I have returned, in which I felt the absence of your presence?

Could home also contain the therapist's office?

The therapist I go to has an office in a house, which is not a house. The house has been turned into a clinic with treatment rooms for various therapies. From the outside, the clinic does not look like a clinic. It is in a street of houses that all look like child's drawings of houses. Most of the houses in the street are homes, but the house across the road from the clinic is also not a house, but a small hotel. Enameled in white pebble-dash, it stands out in the grey street like a capped tooth. From the outside both the clinic and the hotel look exactly like houses.

I could go into one, or the other. Which would cure me?

In the clinic's waiting room there are flowers, just like in a hotel, but they are dried. The walls are white; the curtains are white. There are also chairs arranged, as in a hotel lobby, square against the walls, excusing those who do not want to talk by providing an intimate semblance. But, each time I arrive, I am the only one waiting.

In this waiting room, unlike in a hotel waiting room, which is its lobby, there are no waiters, only me. It is after hours, after work hours. There is no one waiting with me, not even you ("You can come on your own," that's what the therapist told me, "if he doesn't want to come at first, or for every session, or he could just come sometimes, or, otherwise, he could come on his own sometime."). Here, there is no one from whom I might feel the need to escape. Nevertheless, there are magazines—decor, and travel—which ensure that I can leave the waiting room at any time for a world of other places, places the clinic suspects its clients may prefer. I flip through one. Inside, there's a hotel on a cliff in Italy, a loft in Williamsburg, a bothy, or whatever, in Scotland (the word tastes right).

FREUD

[Dora] had been given an album of
views of a German spa town for
Christmas.

In a dream, she escapes into it. It is, Freud thinks, a love token.

In the waiting room, I am waiting. Perhaps, in her room above me, the therapist is waiting too. We are waiting for the appointed hour. We cannot meet before the appointed hour. The waiting room smells of mouthwash as though it were not a therapist's waiting room, but a dentist's, as though what is to be mended here is my mouth as well as my mind. Rinse and spit.

The therapist calls:

"Why don't you come up and see me?"

That sounds funny, like in the movies, like:

MAE WEST

Why don't you come up and see me,
sometime?

Well? Why don't you come up and see me sometime? Why don't you ever come? You could come up sometime, or you could just come sometimes. You could otherwise come up without seeing me. You could have been there at home all the time without seeing me. You could have seen me come in, and decided you'd rather not see me. You know that it's possible.

The therapist wears a shawl that looks like a blanket. Although the weather is hot, she wraps it around herself, a barrier. She says, "You have been through so much." Perhaps I have, but I cannot get through the shawl. I last three sessions before I quit (I'd told her when we began, I'm not looking for sympathy).

What does Freud call it—angst? That's German. Does it translate as anxiety, does it translate as anguish? Anxiety is the feeling of waiting for something bad that is going to happen. It is the feeling that the bad thing is already happening during the waiting, a slow-motion feeling that it will happen nevertheless, and that it will not finish happening until it has got all the way to the end. But it never gets to the end, and the anxiety continues. Anguish comes from the Latin *angustia*, "tensity, tightness" and *angor*, "choking, clogging," and from the ancient Greek ἄγχω (*ankho*) "strangle." Anguish becomes a symptom—perhaps aphonia: its expression, an inability to express anything.

```
              FREUD
  You know you are free to leave any
  time.
```

The one thing I learn in the clinic: *If I express a desire aloud, I immediately think someone will stop me.*

Better keep my mouth shut.

III

FREUD
I began my discussion with a little
experiment which was, as usual,
successful.

Freud asks Dora to look for something on the table that is not usually there. Freud tells us that this is a match holder, a "large" match holder, such as stands on the desk of a hotel lobby. Dora had not noticed it, although "both Herr K and Papa were passionate smokers," as are Freud and Dora herself. The match holder, most likely, contains matches, but, though Freud mentions the box, he says nothing of what is inside. When he asks Dora to look for something, he is asking her to look for the outside, which is what she would see first, if she were looking for the matches. He asks her to look for one aspect of a thing that relates to the whole. This is metonymy.

Freud is always telling me there is something hidden inside something else.

Inside Dora's head is a dream. Freud asks her to relate it. Dora dreams her house will burn down. Her mother wants to save her jewelry; her father becomes angry and insists they leave without it.

Dora's father says, "I don't want me and my two children to burn to death because of your jewellery box."

The fire instructions on the back of my hotel door say, "Assemble in the lobby." They say, "Do not stop to collect any personal goods."

"There was never a real fire at our house," says Dora.

NO SMOKING says the sign on my hotel door. On the back cover of my copy of the Penguin edition of *THE PSYCHOLOGY OF LOVE*, inside which is hidden *DORA, A FRAGMENT OF AN ANALYSIS OF A CASE OF HYSTERIA*, is a photograph of Freud, smoking, posed like Groucho Marx, cigar erect, as though he had just delivered the punchline: "Sometimes a cigar is just a cigar."

Freud did not say this, although many believe he did.

Groucho Marx's most famous joke is, "I wouldn't belong to any club that would have me as a member." Woody Allen, in the opening monologue of his film, *Annie Hall* (1977), says this is "the key joke of my adult life in terms of my relationships with women," and claims that Groucho got it from Freud's *Wit and Its Relation to the Unconscious,* but the joke cannot be found inside Freud's book. In attributing the joke to Freud, Allen may have been mistaken, or he may have been pretending to make a mistake, or he might have been making a mistake knowing it was a mistake all along but was unable, somehow, to keep from making it.

The Groucho version of this joke doesn't occur in any of the Marx Bros. movies. There is no proof Groucho made it. It is attributed to an apocryphal letter of resignation (not a refusal of membership) from—various sources claim—The Friars Club of Beverly Hills, The Delaney Club, The Lambs

Club, The Beverly Hills Tennis Club, or The Hillcrest Country Club. The story was first repeated in Erskine Johnson's syndicated Hollywood gossip column,[1] in 1949. Ten years later, Groucho recycled the story in his memoir, in which he claims to have sent a telegram: "PLEASE ACCEPT MY RESIGNATION. I DON'T WANT TO BELONG TO ANY CLUB THAT WILL ACCEPT ME AS A MEMBER." There is no proof the telegram was ever sent. Dora would not accept the fact that she did not mention the matches as proof that her silence also concealed a desire for Herr K's member. Though Freud suggested this, she would not even speak of it.

So Freud did not say the thing about the cigar, and he did not say the thing about the member. But then nor, perhaps, did Groucho. And Mae West did not say, "Why don't you come up and see me sometime." She said, "Why don't you come up sometime and see me." It's just we prefer to remember all these jokes otherwise. And, when I google, it appears that Hardy never said, "That's another fine mess you've got me into," and Nelson did not say, "Kiss me, Hardy." All the best lines seem to be anon.

Rudyard Kipling really did say, in a poem called "The Betrothed," "A woman is only a woman, but a good cigar is a smoke."

Some sources tell me that Groucho Marx said that too, though it seems unlikely.

Groucho did say (to a father of seventeen children, on a game show): "I love my cigar too, but I take it out of my mouth once in a while."

Or did he say it to a woman?

Who had nine children?

Or is this just another urban myth?

Sometimes a cigar is just a cigar, but a good woman is a . . . What?

"We can substitute a box for this," says Freud. "A box and a woman go better together."

Janet Malcolm, in her essays on psychoanalysis, "The Impossible Profession," calls this a "feat of ratiocination." Malcolm says that Freud thought Dora was Pandora, but, in her dream, Dora shows no interest in the box.

```
              FREUD
            (To Dora)
So far you've talked about the
jewellery and said nothing about a
box.
```

Freud shows no interest in the matches in the match stand. He only mentions the box. And Freud never tells us exactly why he wanted Dora to notice the box, and what was successful about his experiment.

Although Dora and her father suffer in the lungs, the throat, the mouth, no one, in Freud's story, becomes sick from smoking.

Freud died from cancer of the jaw, attributed to his cigar habit.

"There is," said Freud, "*no smoke without fire.*"

Or maybe that is a misquote.[2]

Groucho fictionalized the name of the club that would have had him for a member, which makes it more difficult to attempt to verify his telegram. Whether he really sent it is anybody's guess. In later life, Groucho complained that he was unable to satisfactorily insult anyone because they always thought it was a joke. Freud fictionalized all the names in his *Case of Hysteria*, so that none of the characters could be recognized in real life.

Except himself.

IV

A FRIEND
Don't question marriage. Once the box
has been opened . . .

There were a few times I put our marriage box on the fire, but never quite set it alight. Inside were photographs, dried roses, cards of congratulation from dead people, cards of congratulation from people I'd never see again, cards from people who had turned into altogether different people since we were married. I hadn't wanted roses. It wasn't the season for the flowers I did want. The box was made of card and contained mainly paper. It would have burnt well.

Dora left Freud before the term of her treatment was up. Although she gave him notice, he still found this unexpected.

> FREUD
>
> ```
> She seemed to be moved; she said
> goodbye to me very warmly, with the
> heartiest wishes for the new year,
> and—came no more.
> ```

To leave, wrote Freud, was "undoubtedly an act of revenge on her part," but Janet Malcolm said this was just "transference burn."

> FREUD
>
> ```
> What are transferences? They are new
> editions, facsimiles, of the impulses
> and fantasies that are to be awakened,
> and rendered conscious as the analysis
> progresses.
> ```

Something is happening in relation to desire. I'm not sure whose. Dora's sought in Freud (Freud claimed) "a substitute for the tenderness she longed for." This is transference. Freud's interest in Dora meant, perhaps, that she resembled something he longed for too. What?

Metonymy is something close to an object, a shorthand, something more convenient, as close as a box is to what is inside it. Freud found that the patient can become attached to the therapist because he is nearer to hand, and in some way resembles what is longed for, but, says Malcolm, also vice versa. When Dora felt a constriction in her throat, Freud may have longed for Dora to mean *penis*. Transference, says Freud, is not a cure, but can be a stage in a cure.

My hotels do not resemble the home I long for, as I do not long for home. They do not resemble anything that can be longed for. They may resemble a longing for home, but they do not satisfy it.

3 MARRIAGE POSTCARDS

"The patient's inability to give an ordered description of her life history, insofar as it coincides with the case history . . ."

—SIGMUND FREUD, *DORA: A FRAGMENT OF A CASE OF HYSTERIA*

```
Cast:
Sigmund Freud:        a psychoanalyst
Dora:                 a teenage girl
```

Postcard #1—Postcards

(This postcard shows the hotel from the sea: it must have been taken from a boat.)

I have felt for a long while, maybe forever, that there is something not right about my life. The plot could be better, or maybe the scenery. This is, perhaps, why I am writing. I have suspected for a while that some people talk to the page because there is no one else they can talk to any more.

```
             FREUD
From my time in Charcot's clinic I
remembered seeing and hearing that
among people with hysterical mutism,
writing vicariously stood in for
speech. They wrote fluently, more
quickly, and better than other people
did.[1]
```

In the drawer in the faux-leather-topped desk in my hotel room, is a faux-leather folder. Inside, blank pages with the hotel's address, a single envelope, and one postcard showing the hotel's facade. Here I am on the inside of the hotel, which cannot be seen on the postcard. A temporary address, I am safe. I'm not giving anything away.

People write from hotels. Once there, what else is there to do?

Postcard #2—Writing

(This postcard shows the front of the hotel, which is tipped at an angle so the entire facade can be included.)

If I were inventing, as a writer, such
a mental state for a novella . . .

Here in the hotel, it is difficult to think what was bad about home. To turn over the bad bits is still surprising.

There are a lot of facts, all contradictory, as facts are.

A lot of opinions, then?

Yes, even within the same heads.

As soon as I leave home, I can't remember what happened there.

I write the words over, and the facts change.

I do not know how to put them in order. I do not know if these things can be ordered.

I do not know exactly what it is I know.

I do not know exactly what it is I'll write.

Since I left, I have felt my honesty changing completely. I begin to forget what happened. How much you—I—did wrong. Perhaps it was not so very much. Perhaps it was as little as I would have liked, nearly as little as is conversant with what would have been acceptable. Yes, I did not do wrong things very often, though when I did, it was with a purpose, which I can define, not with the need to possess all of you, to get right inside the wrong things that you were doing. Which is of course what I did want.

What did I want?

Was it ever only one thing?

Postcard #3—Silence

(This postcard does not show the hotel at all, but a nearby monument and, printed underneath, the name of the hotel.)

Marriage functions so two people live beside each other in ways that allow them not to touch or communicate too directly, in quiet.

Inquiet.

Dora wrote a message she did not send. Her parents found a letter "in or on the girl's desk, in which she bade them farewell because her life had become unbearable."

> DORA
> It was locked in my desk.

> FREUD
> I conclude that she had played it into their hands herself.

I leave my g-chat window open, in case you want to get in touch.

Sometimes, when it looks like you're there, you don't answer.

I never wanted the strong and silent type.

I have to learn to shut up.

If I don't talk, if things went on as before, you would forgive me.

But I don't want things to go on as before.

Not speaking, we go on, somehow, still, sometimes using words.

Your green light has gone. You have safely logged out. I'm safe now, safe from my desire for you, which I no longer at any point desire.

To speak to you is immediately to feel anxious I've said the wrong thing.

Perhaps because I have.

If I express a desire aloud, I immediately think someone will stop me.

Postcard #4—Dora time

(This postcard shows the intimate view of the hotel's interior court from the eye level of a swimmer in the hotel pool.)

                    DORA
    [I] asked about a hundred times,
    "Where is the station?"

                  EVERYONE
    Five minutes.

Dora dreams she is trying to get to the railway station. She asks for an answer in streets, she is given an answer in minutes. Space presents as time. Home is a matter of years. Sometimes when I'm temporary, my eye lifts to the hotel cornicing and meets an architrave, unexpected. When I get used to this, it seems odd to wake up in the same place every day.

Time is particularly important in *A Case of Hysteria*—fourteen days, two and a half hours, nine months—but locations—a spa, a town, a railway station—are imprecise.

> DORA
> (Dreams)
> I am going for a walk in a town I
> don't know. I see streets and squares
> that are strange to me.

Why so precise about time and so vague about place?

"Where do you want to go this weekend?" you used to ask me sometimes. That's a question I never asked myself. My time was taken up with all the things I had to do. Now I can go anywhere.

Postcard #5—Clock time

(This postcard does not show the hotel, but the view from the hotel, across the harbor.)

When you are on the other side of the world from me, when, sometimes, you are in one hotel and I am in another, or when one of us is at home and the other is not, I know how long a night takes, and it doesn't take long: from 3:00 p.m. to 9:00 p.m., maybe. I know that it is exactly two minutes past seven where you are, and that something has happened between us today while we were apart, and that when I think of you I feel it, but I cannot remember exactly what it was.

Hotel time is flat. Today is approaching from all sides.

I'm not so good with time. If you cancel something 'til Thursday it's so far ahead it's impossible to imagine. Time stops when I hear music, when I'm walking, when I'm drinking, when I'm with you, or someone. . . . So many things can stop the clocks; so I don't care about them anymore. I think that's called ecstasy.

Postcard #6—Anxiety time

(*This postcard shows a view of the hotel from the beach. The hotel is distant and hidden behind some palm trees.*)

I am not happy. The reason I am not happy triangulates. I am not happy with you (you should change), or I am unhappy with the powerlessness of my unhappiness with you, which means I am unhappy with myself. Perhaps I should have therapy to change myself, or to change my attitude to you. You are unimprovable, as you refuse to visit therapy with me, or alone. Then I am unhappy with my unhappiness with myself, because it is powerless to prompt in you the unhappiness with yourself that would lead you to wish to change. So my unhappiness shifts back to my circumstances which, were I not so unhappy with myself—were I able to treat myself as a person I am not so unhappy with—I could change.

One thing I am happy with is how good I am at being unhappy.

Postcard #7—Married time

(This postcard is a black-and-white photo of the hotel as it was 100 years ago.)

The marriage registrar told us to say, *I will*, but said we wanted to say, *I do*, like in the movies, in the continuous present (though, of course, this is something we said in the past).

The anxiety around marriage takes place at its borders. If everyone making a home together could be "married," where are the limits of its promise? I don't know how to define marriage. I know it's a thing. I just don't know what it's for. Or, maybe it doesn't matter what it's for, it's just, I don't know how it manifests. It always seems about to manifest. I strain my eyes to a point on the horizon.

Perhaps married is a "from," not a "to." Maybe that's why I can't see the point.

Or is marriage a destination *and* a starting point, like a hotel, which is both.

Who was it said, "If it doesn't work out, you can always get divorced"? It looks like a Roy Lichtenstein but it was Douglas Coupland in that book, a hymn to our generation (X). "Don't worry, mother, if the marriage doesn't work out we can always get divorced," says a black-and-white blonde, holding a steaming cup of coffee to her lips, no mother in the frame, no husband. As though it were up to her.

Legally I can check out any time, but it's not easy to leave my desire for it.

Postcard #8—Home times

(This postcard is oriented in landscape and split vertically into two unequal panels. 80 percent of the postcard shows a view of the hotel front, 20 percent shows a man and a woman on skis. They are taller than the hotel.)

If marriage is "from," home is "to." Home would be when we had accumulated all its parts. Once we lived in a house where only one room was livable, where the others had holes in the floor, the walls. For a while there was no heating, for a while there was no water. Was that home? Not at that moment, but we were working on it. It didn't matter that home was not there yet, that we slept on a mattress, cooked in a microwave, that I fed the baby on bare boards. We lived at a low level, sitting on the floor. The other rooms were filled with furniture turned in upon itself. We didn't seem to need it. The house did not look like home then but it was. Home was in hope. I don't hope for home any more.

(Is there no place we can be together except the future?)

Postcard #9—Me-time

(This postcard shows the hotel frontage but, in order that it fills the height of the picture, it is cut off at either side.)

I can scarcely begin to say what went on between us. It was so mundane its violence is embarrassing. All I can say is it is not going on now, so I can no longer describe it.

It was to do with self.

It was to do with where I was, myself, which was a problem not only of space but also of time.

It was a problem, like marriage, like home, of prepositions. Who am I *for*? That's the question I kept asking. If I'm not for you, who am I for? I knew I shouldn't want to be for someone: I should be living for art, perhaps. I should be living for myself, or whatever, and, yes, I tried to desire these abstracts.

I have an adhesible yearning, reuseble as blu-tac.

Perhaps I will always be looking for something better.

As soon as I think of a man, I begin to lose myself.

Postcard #10—Bedtime

(This postcard shows a bush that might be in the hotel's garden. In front of the bush stands a woman in a white dress, one hand on her hip, the other in her hair. She is looking off to the left, away from the hotel's name, which appears in white cursive lettering on the right.)

Since bed and board constitute
marriage.

I needed help with the beds. At home, often, the end of the day would come and still not all the beds had been made. Some beds returned to night without their sheets ever having been straightened. This was not the way it should be—but who should do it for them? They couldn't do it for themselves. They were weak in the head, they were infants, they needed a mother, they needed a nurse, they needed a maid. I did not want to be it, but who else was there so conveniently wearing an apron?

There is something about a mown lawn that is like a made bed. Evidence of work I didn't have to do. A made bed is my province; a mown lawn is yours. In order to exact work from you, I must do mine. I like the feeling that something has been done for me, even if I dislike the work I must do in exchange. And I must do it every day whereas a lawn must be mown once a fortnight at most, less frequently in winter. But how much I like the smell of new-mown grass, of fresh-washed sheets.

Postcard #11—Home work

(*This portrait-oriented postcard is split horizontally, approximately 50/50. The top panel shows the front of the hotel, the bottom a hotel room. The building seems to balance on the curtain rail.)*

Some things to do with home cannot be taught, but can only be learned through experience (or, these things never come into words, or else words never come into it). Home is an art, the way that knowing the grain in wood is an art, like knowing how to cut a board to make a bed. The art of most people is home.

Because we both had other arts, it was difficult to pursue the art of home. For most people it is difficult to pursue two difficult things. Usually it is enough for one partner to pursue home. This is usually the woman. The other person, usually the man, can look on approvingly, seeing home is being made, though not by him. This is home work.

Home work is a work done behind closed doors. Unlike cutting a board to make a bed, it leaves no evidence. Time is undone each time the bed is made up. Home work—cleaning, ironing, washing—is undoing.

And, for your part, you liked to look on and approve. On the children, on the animals, with which we filled home, and who required in their turn beds made of board, which was one action, and the continual making and unmaking of those beds, which was another. You liked to see me look after them. You allowed yourself this look, no doubt with the best intentions, with the intention of looking on my home work approvingly. If I didn't do the home work right your look changed. You could hardly help yourself, but it was awful to be looked on, even when your look was approving.

It built a wall between us that did not look like a wall, like the glass wall in a television set; I was inside, you were outside. I was constrained to act, by duty, by sympathy (by love?), constrained by your looking to go on doing. You, perhaps, were constrained by my actions to keep on looking, though your action involved only yourself. I was lonely, demonstrating my prowess at home work, with only the children, the animals for company. My work was looked at, but I could not look at yours—a TV screen is one-way. I'm not sure you were lonely: you always had someone to look at. This is called looking after.

You never know how your wife will work out, so you look after her home work very carefully. You can marry a sensible woman, give her a home, and she will become unreasonable. She might demand a hotel.

Postcard #12—Part-time

(This postcard shows a view onto the hotel pool, from a window that might be in the hotel.)

Since we parted, when I am on my own with my home work, knowing that you are not looking as it is no longer your role to look, I am perfectly content. I could be making a home for myself. If you arrived I would no longer feel at home; I would be on edge. I would think you should look after the work I had done, and, in order to show it to you, I would have to work in a way you might want to look at. If you were at home, but not looking, I would be anxious: that you did not want to look, that you did not want to participate in home even by looking. I needed the looking. If you did not look, it was not work. If it was not work, it had no beginning and no end. If you did not look, my home work had no boundaries.

Watching me, this home-making must have seemed eccentric: an animal building by instinct, from sticks, debris, its own fur and bodily fluids. No one knows why.

No one asked me to do it, did they?

Perhaps.

Postcard #–11 — Away

(This postcard is divided into six squares, five of which show ancient monuments, the sixth, the hotel.)

Rewind. I am at home. My soon-to-be-ex husband is away. Like two wooden people on a cuckoo clock, one is in when the other is out. The whole day has been calm. I had forgotten how calm home could be. The more I wriggle toward divorce the more painful I know it will be, the closer I get to the terrible blank pain I felt yesterday when I realized I had persuaded you to leave, calm panic with no prospect of an end. But the more I work my way toward it determinedly, the more triumphant I feel. I do not understand, nor can I predict, what I want. I can trust only the leaving. It must happen. It is happening already.

Did I spend all my time waiting for the moment you'd be gone? And, now you have, will I wait hopelessly for your return? Wanting you gone is such a delicate mechanism. How much of you, even absent, there is from which to defend myself. I'd looked forward for weeks to your departure. No more holding my breath in the evenings, hearing you breathing in the other room. Perhaps I will even use the other room to read my books.

Now that I no longer have you, I no longer have the kind of loneliness in which to wait for you. I no longer have to wait, but I have not yet developed the leisure to read a book. It is a different kind of loneliness. Perhaps, at first, it is worse.

I will shepherd my melancholy, turn it into something else. I'll have to. Learn this other kind of loneliness: you won't be seeing him again.

Postcard #–10—Pockets

(*This postcard shows a model on a generic beach, her back turned to us, the hotel's name below her deck chair. The hotel is a chain hotel. This branch does not have a beach.*)

Rewind. One of marriage's hidden violences of thought. When you were away I liked to look through your pockets. Perhaps I would find some kind of evidence of something, I don't know what. It's a husband who has pockets and who has things to put into them. My pockets are small, sometimes stitched (a reminder that anything I put in would spoil the line). I seldom put things in my pockets but you overstuffed yours: receipts, notes, parking fines of many months' passing. You wore through the bottom of your pockets until things fell into the linings of your clothes.

Whatever I found there, it never told me anything about you.

Postcard #–9—Drunk time

(This postcard shows a hotel bathroom. It is empty.)

Rewind: At home, I'd lurch toward drunk twice a week, sometimes more. Always I did it while waiting. And, when I did, I could smell the moldiness, that particular floral *eau de javel*, whatever, that is more rotten than rotten. It's either decay, or its opposite. But I don't need to drink as much now you are not here. I don't fret in the evenings that you are doing something alone when you could be doing something companionable, though I am reading here alone, as usual, and in bed. I am allowed to. I disapproved of what you did with your evenings. Each harmless thing you did seemed an affront.

I had forgotten that I am allowed to be divorced. Here in the provinces, I know no divorced people. A friend in London emailed, wrote, Oh, all my friends are doing it. And I felt normal again.

Postcard #–8—Evening

(This postcard shows half a gilt-framed mirror. The rest of the postcard has the hotel's address. I have not seen a mirror like this in the hotel.)

Rewind: Tears left me with a headache—or is it the cold? I sought the illusion of companionship and thought it would be okay, you and me at home working side by side at work that was not home work. Instead I found that you made noises and I made noises, and they were wrong noises. Perhaps it's okay not to know each other, to preserve unknowing. Perhaps that's what marriage is. We stopped working. I read. You watched TV.

I used to be unable to sleep in the same bed as you. Then I was unable to eat at the same table. There was always somewhere I was not doing something with you.

Not a good night, then, nor the couple of nights before. And the bad nights still outnumber the good nights. And keeping notebooks means discontent, and discontent means writing.

Postcard #–7—Married time II

(This postcard is a view across a hotel room from the made bed to the window. The window has net curtains. The photographer could be sitting on the bed.)

Rewind: Tonight you went for a drink after work. I had already been looking after our children and their friends for a long while. I had noticed the clock five minutes, two minutes, before, then two minutes, five minutes, fifteen minutes, half an hour after. When you got in touch I acquiesced, politely, and asked if you would like to stay out later. That's marriage, I guess. We have to make room for each other. I am in a room, at home, and you are not. Tonight I am having a married experience and you are not, as you would also go out for a drink with colleagues if you were not married, but I would not be here in this room if I were not. Marriage is our constraints in relation to each other. Married time is time with the corners trimmed off.

You told me:

You have it better than other women.

Or was it:

Other women have it worse than you?

You never asked if I had it better or worse than other men.

Or whether I have it better or worse than you.

Postcard #–6—Angry time

(This postcard shows the hotel's rooftop pool: it is empty.)

You tell me you want to be with me.

You only tell me that when you are not here.

When you are not here, you do not tell me where you are or when you will be coming back.

That would be okay, if we weren't "together."

We are "together" but we are seldom together.

You say we spend all our time together.

We are frequently at home together, but seldom in the same room.

Home contains not being together; it is essential to it.

Here I am at home where you are not. I stink of home—is that why you won't come near me? I hate what home has made of me. I hate the home that we have made.

You have left me with home to care for. It is your home as well as mine. I have not made this home alone. I don't mind home work. I mind that you don't see it. I don't ask that you help me, I only ask that you see me doing it. I gave up asking for help a long time ago. Now, I ask for nothing, and you are able to give me less than nothing.

Give her a home. Who is it gives the home to the other?

Because home is measured in time, not space, you will give it to me again.

You might give it to me every day.

It is rational that this should obsess me. Given my position, I am allowed to be obsessed by this.

A reasonable wife would leave you alone.

A reasonable wife would be at home with your not being at home. When she is at home, she is married. When she is absent from home, she is not married. When she is at home, not being married is absent from her: she is absent from part of herself. She is absent from it all the time she is there.

Postcard #–5—Leaving time

(This postcard shows the hotel dining room: no one is eating there.)

> *FREUD*
> *There are cases with purely internal motives such as self-punishment, regret and atonement.*

Dora can leave Herr K; she can leave her father.

If she leaves, she cannot grant herself enjoyment (or acknowledgment) of her desires, as they involve the people she is leaving.

But she cannot leave her time and she cannot go far from her place and, although she may love the people who want her, she has no control over how she is wanted.

Dora, instead, denies Freud the continuation of their conversation.

She wants everyone (Herr K, Frau K, her father) to go back to their own homes. In wanting that she is, perhaps, like her mother.

I also wanted everything to be just so. As everything was not, I was wrong, perhaps, to desire it.

What happens when someone leaves who is part of the structure of every day?

Postcard #–4—Nameless

(This postcard shows a line drawing of the hotel. The hotel's walls fade out before they get to the building next door.)

We went into marriage to fulfil our individual desires (as we had been told we were individuals), but we found ourselves required to be fulfilled by what we found there, which is no more than what other people have found. The marriage problem is the same as the hotel problem.

I have second-guessed your desires, and those of others. I have made myself into a hotel.

Postcard #–3—Nameless II

(This postcard shows neither the hotel, nor any nearby view: it shows a color graphic of a surfer.)

I wish I could find a good analyst, one who could help me find a way out. Some friends say they have good ones, but they live elsewhere. I can't keep on trying. For financial reasons, for emotional reasons, I need some commitment; I need to commit to someone. I wish I could find a good analyst like I wish I could find a good husband. I don't wish it like I wish I could find a good home. I don't wish to find a good home any more. If I could be married without a home, perhaps that would work.

Postcard #–2—Ending

(This postcard shows some cliffs above the sea. There is no hotel in the photograph that may, or may not, have been taken from the hotel.)

I email you about an email I didn't send.
I email you about not sending the email.
-It was not bad email.
-Good.
-but still didn't send.
-Why not?

If I am talking to you again does that mean there was never any story?

Plot is good in books but bad in life. Plot is like angst: the fear that something bad is about to happen—is already happening. Why not go backward? There is no plot in a hotel so nothing very bad can happen here. When I am in a hotel, the bad thing that will happen is in abeyance but it is waiting to happen somewhere outside the hotel nevertheless. Meanwhile (while I am in the hotel) nothing will come to an end. I am struggling toward ending. I have left you but the ending is still not arriving. Endings do not arrive in hotels.

I cannot end this. I thought I had ended things already. Why can I not end this?

Postcard #–1 — Returning

(Like other postcards in many of the faux-leather folders in the hotels I have stayed in, this one shows a hotel room with the double bed, unoccupied.)

Rewind: I woke at 3:00 a.m. in a hotel and bought a plane ticket back home.

If I go back, I thought, I will have a home. I won't have to worry about the rent. I won't have to worry about getting a haircut. I can buy new clothes at the beginning of each season instead of waiting for the sales. I can—I will—buy from the designer boutique I like one jacket, one pair of trousers, and a dress. These things will cost—how much? So long as spending does not become a habit it will be nothing.

In the airport shop I tried a cream that promised to erase the pouches under my eyes that came from all that hotel crying. The cream cost—how much? Much more than I would spend on myself. If I wanted, I could have bought that too.

It would have been nothing, nothing . . .

£72.00 for a plane ticket.

It is very little.

Later that week I met F in the supermarket—divorced. She asked whether we were back together. I said, yes, but. . . . Before I could finish, she told me this was good. I don't know why she should say this.

I remember, before meeting you, how optimistic I was about how love would be.

Despite everything I still feel exactly the same.

4 HOMETEL

"He failed to sing of a region for living"
**—MALLARMÉ'S "LE CYGNÉ," TRANSLATED BY ANNE
CARSON IN *THE ALBERTINE WORKOUT***

```
Cast:
Martin Heidegger:    a philosopher
Sigmund Freud:       a psychoanalyst
Odysseus:            a guest/homeowner
Someone:             a friend(?)
The Library Hotel:   a hotel
```

I

```
                  HEIDEGGER
What if man's homelessness consisted
in this, that man still does not even
think of the real plight of dwelling
as the plight? Yet as soon as man
```

gives thought to his homelessness,
it is a misery no longer. Rightly
considered and kept well in mind, it
is the sole summons that calls mortals
into their dwelling.

There was a time just after we got married when it was fashionable to have your home look like a hotel. What did a hometel look like? We saw it in magazines. It was white, mainly, and clean, and spare. Hard, dark surfaces—wood and slate—were overlaid with things that were pale and soft. In these pictures of homes that looked like hotels, there were no guests. The rooms were ready; only they were absent.

I had looked forward to making a home—but not one I'd lived in. An Ideal Home? Perhaps. Not knowing what to desire other than what I'd seen, I wondered: could hotel come to me?

Our first home was rented, furnished. Having nothing already we filled it with the presents we found waiting on our wedding night. Someone with a car had dropped them off and, before going to bed, we unwrapped them. The presents were wrapped in silver and white paper and they were mostly white and silver: plates, cups, pans, a pair of candlesticks. We had sex that night, yes, in a heap of discarded tissue, but we unwrapped the presents first. We'd had sex before, but we had never had such things!

Home is accumulation: the rush of possessions. Some homes are a whole history in objects: college students return to flick through their toddler books, parents kick past their children's outgrown shoes. This hanging on to things is what makes it home, where dates are reckoned from a crack in the teapot. Some families live like this, but I wanted none of it. I didn't want to be responsible for things. You liked to keep things, I liked to throw them away—a wrapper, a receipt, a piece of paper, an old file (to make room for something else? I don't know what). There's always something to get rid of. But I also liked to spend time in other people's homes, the kind where people kept things. I liked to float, dateless myself, anchored to other people's dates.

At home we tried to get things right but, before everything was in place, parts started to deteriorate, things chipped before we got other things that went with them. You, especially, were left behind. Or was it me? Things can look better weathered, but ours never wore properly. Funny how things never wear in quite the right places.

There were things that went into the house at the beginning of our marriage that may never leave: forks, tin openers, pans, chairs. If I leave, some of these things will leave with me; beds will come blinking into the clear day. It seems unfair to drag them out—their scarred legs, their wrinkled bedspreads—half dead, into the light.

In hotels, things come and go frequently, and nothing there is shabby, unless it's shabby chic. Things from home seldom go into hotels, though it often happens the other way round. Some things go out of hotels and into home, the small things that come for free, like shampoo, like soap (or, rather, they are included in the price). But a guest would not take the lamps, the rugs, the pictures, no, though some do remove the robes, the bath towels, the ashtrays. Some people I know collect these things, displaying them in their own bathrooms or, more often, guest rooms, so their guests feel they might not be at home, but in a hotel.

Thinking about things happens when I have some distance on them. In a hotel I have some distance on how things are at home, but I have no distance from the things in the hotel. Although some of them are the same things I have at home, I don't react to them in at all the same way as I do there. Where else but in hotels are things so entirely different—so disposable, and so much worshipped? Being full of things that are replaced as soon as they stop working as part of the whole, a hotel is a thing in itself. In a hotel, everything must be just so.

II

For our second home (mortgaged, unfurnished) I bought: white sheets, beige armchairs, white curtains. He bought a red sofa. I was frightened. I painted the walls in a shade called Elephant's Breath. He bought a rug with stripes the color of coromandel. I bought a white rug for the bedroom. It was impractical. He bought white kitchen units. They showed every speck. I was a lady in the drawing room, he was a lady in the kitchen, where I was the cook, but he was not. We were both whores, perhaps, but not necessarily in the bedroom.

That red sofa. He made the first mark, blood-colored. I carried blood with me all the time. From time to time I let it out, which was not practical with all that beige. My friend (female, older, visiting) said, "Why is there blood in the toilet?" I looked at the white porcelain, said, "Well, it must have been me." She was—temporarily—mystified. The sheets in the hotels I visited were always white, no matter what color the covers. In one hotel, I bled on the white sheets, rinsed them under the showerhead and dried them with the hairdryer. I had a duty to the hotel, a duty not to be too human.

FREUD

The pride taken by women in the appearance of their genitals is quite a special feature of their vanity; and disorders of the genitals which they think calculated to inspire feelings of repugnance or even disgust have an incredible power of humiliating them.[1]

In a hotel, which is ideal, I too am ideal.

You were always reluctant to go to hotels. Now I know why.

Still, I feel better lying here alone in my hotel, than I would talking to someone who doesn't want to be talked to, across the white hotel stretches of sheet and table cloth.

At home I stripped the covers off the bed. It looked nude. It was no longer white. And there were our negatives imprinted in its dirty flesh. They were no longer ours. At home, our temporary shadows smudged themselves across the permanent furniture. They got shorter as the years got longer. You would have thought the opposite, that, as the proportion of our lives increased as a percentage of the lives of our books, our pans, our plates, the bricks and mortar of our home, we'd have made some mark upon it, but these objects showed no sign of diminishing, and our shadows, which seemed at first to grow longer, wore themselves out across them, and shrank as the sun moved across the day.

Move a chair, and the room looks temporary.

III

HEIDEGGER
We do not dwell because we have built,
but we build and have built because
we dwell, that is, because we are
dwellers.

Bauen (German: to build), Heidegger tells us in his essay "Building, Dwelling, Thinking," also means "to dwell" but the English word "dwell" is not related to "to build." Dwell, says Webster's Dictionary (1913) means:

1   To delay; to linger.

2   To abide; to remain; to continue.

Synonyms.—To inhabit; live; abide; sojourn; reside; continue; stay; rest.

In English, dwell is an *unheimlich* word, a word that contains its opposite. The word comes from the Old English *dwellan*, "to lead astray, hinder, delay" (in Middle English "to tarry, remain in a place"). It is a word of Germanic origin, a word related to Middle Dutch *dwellen* "to stun, perplex" and Old Norse *dvelja* "delay, tarry, stay."

Old English *dwellan* also means "to mislead, deceive," originally "to make a fool of," from Proto-Germanic *dwelan* (cognates: Old Norse *dvöl* "delay," *dvali* "sleep"; Old High German *twellen* "to hinder, delay"; Danish *dvale* "trance, stupor," *dvaelbær* "narcotic berry," a source of Middle English *dwale* "nightshade"), from Proto Indo-European *dhwel-*, extended form of root *dheu-* "dust, cloud, vapor, smoke" (and related notions of "defective perception or wits"). Related to Old English *gedweola* "error, heresy, madness." The sense shifted in Middle English through "hinder, delay," to "linger" (c.1200, as still in phrase *to dwell upon*), to "make a home" (mid-13c.). Related: *Dwelled*; *dwelt*; *dwells*.[2]

It seems we dwell through force, or through deception. It seems ("to lead astray," "to stun") that dwell is something we do not do, but something that is done to us. We are dwelt on.

You don't have to be mad to live here, but it helps . . .

IV

This thinking of homelessness, rather than bemoaning the absence of a home, concerns itself with the presence within our homes of that which cannot be thought.

Home. How could I think of living anywhere else? Other places exist only to show you how good it is. These places might be technicolor, but technicolor isn't—what?—sustainable? Home, like in the hometel magazines, is in black and white. *There's no place like home*, and if you say it three times you'll be there. But in order to say it you have to be not-there. You can only think about home from elsewhere.

From my hotel I think of my home, which asked so much of me that I could no longer think. I was not at home with thinking there, was always busy doing, though, whatever I did, it never felt like I was building anything. We lived there for a long time. All of our building went on there. Now I can't think what color the door was.

There are parts of home I have already forgotten, the parts I thought of as yours. I don't go into them anymore. Even to think of going into them would mean more work. You will not do the work. You will notice if I do it, but you won't think twice.

It's not the not-working, it's then not-thinking. Sometimes you treat this place like a hotel!

I must think of the unthinkable: The hotel in home.

V

HEIDEGGER

```
Mortals dwell in that they await the
divinities as divinities. In hope they
hold up to the divinities what is
unhoped for. They wait for intimations
of their coming and do not mistake the
signs of their absence. They do not
make their gods for themselves and do
not worship idols. In the very depth
of misfortune they wait for the weal
that has been withdrawn.
```

Xenia was the ancient Greek practice of hospitality to strangers, of making your home into a hotel, but without expectation of payment. The word comes from the visiting god's name—Zeus Xenios in his incarnation as the god of travelers—and from *Xenos*, which means stranger in every state, from guest to enemy. To be hospitable, to be hostile: both involve strangers. Odysseus, for example, returned to his own home, disguised, begging for shelter.

ODYSSEUS

For I too once dwelt in a house of my own among men, a rich man in a wealthy house, and full often I gave gifts to a wanderer, whosoever he was and with whatsoever need he came.[3]

A god (a Greek god, at least) is a stranger in the house. Home is where god is not. It is private even from god, who must arrive in disguise to discover what goes on there. The god who visits, dwells with us in the Old English sense, that is, he makes a fool of us. The uncanny, said Freud, is the return of the familiar in a new guise. Zeus Xenios appears, disguised, tests his hosts for virtue, then throws off his cloak. How passive-aggressive! Yet I'd always hoped to be a host, perhaps to have a witness to the work I'd done. We'd have parties, I'd imagined, visitors. Our home would have been open, we'd have entertained angels. And, if we had, how many times might we have found god (or, how many times would he have gone unrecognized)?

To fear a guest as I would fear god, though? No. god is surely not a hotel inspector, and no houseguest would treat your home like a hotel. *Xenia* also involves guesthood. The guest must respect, must not bother the host. A home is somewhere you learn to pick up after yourself . . . or after others, like a Christian god, who is everywhere, and is more like the chambermaid or, perhaps, the hotel detective.

```
                    SOMEONE
    (A friend? Mine? Yours? I can't
    remember.)
    You were neither of you home makers.
```

No, we were both guests.

They should have laid it out, the gods, for home too: the tariff, some kind of prenup. As it was, we made each other welcome, leaving no messages on the pillows, nothing complimentary but an exchange.

Xenia was an exchange, though Greek hosts paid it forward, their reward held in abeyance, to be claimed at another time, in another place, and possibly by others who were nevertheless their avatars. The Greek gods never stayed in hotels. Having *Xenia*, hotels were not needed. But a Christian god is now in service. In Christian charity he asks us to give with no expectation of exchange, so someone has to take up the slack.

Hotels take me out of *Xenia*, out of charity. How relaxing. In a hotel, I can forget the rules, bathe in champagne, throw my TV out the window. No one cares how I behave, so long as I can pay.

When we'd paid it off, I'd go, that's what I thought. Paid for our home, I mean, the mortgage, then we'd owe each other nothing. But we paid it off, and I didn't go, not immediately. Then, several months after, I did.

VI

A building does not have to be for dwelling. A hotel is not for dwelling in the German sense, though it might be in the English, in the sense of a word that contains its inverse. A hotel is for staying in, but it is a kind of staying that includes its opposite: leaving. We may dwell in a hotel in the English sense, in the sense that while we stay there we might also be stunned, led astray, drugged, or made fools of. We know our stay there is temporary, so we do not think to build our futures there. A home which I inhabit as a building but in which I see no future, so in which I do not dwell, and yet, unlike a hotel, which I cannot easily leave, is no situation I could build on.

It was not easy to leave, and when I left, I looked for other homes, anything so long as they didn't look like homes. I looked at a houseboat (all I could afford, I thought, or wanted to) but the owner's cigarette smoke was sunk deep in its timbers. I looked at homes in warehouses, garages, stables; I looked at tiny houses built in corridors between semis, one room on each floor, the bedroom in the loft. In every marital bedroom, in every home I visited, by each marital bed without exception, a shelf of self-help books: sex, relationships, family, money sometimes. By the bed! In some homes, no books elsewhere, except, occasionally, food books in the kitchen. These are the books even people who don't read books will pay for.

Well, we all need a little self-help. I shouldn't dwell on it.

VII

In the Library Hotel and Wellness resort in Cypress, which I have not visited, there is a room called the Martin Heidegger room.

Wellness?

> FREUD
> One need only turn each individual
> reproach back on the person of the
> speaker.

The Library Hotel encourages its guests to help themselves.

> THE LIBRARY HOTEL
> House guests can elevate their spirit
> while experiencing wellbeing of
> body and soul at the Wellness Baths
> designed for total self care.

Most visitors like the Library Hotel. Of those who don't, some complain that the amenities are poor, but that the service is good. Others like the hotel but blame the staff.

TRIPADVISOR:

(A POST)

```
Wrote a complaint, no response, these
people are amateurs and completely
clueless.
```

VIII

Heidegger did not travel much. But neither did he stay at home. He had a hut on a hill, which looked, to be honest, quite luxurious—more like a chalet, the kind you go to on holiday, with several rooms, and probably some source of heating and somewhere to cook. He worked there and, I think, slept and ate there too. He did not call this home, though. He called it his hut.

TRIPADVISOR: A POST:

```
I am travelling to Europe this sept
and want to make a special effort to
go to todtnauberg just to take a look
at heidegger's hut. I know its private
property but I would be happy to look
at the outside.
```

Is it better to look at something private from the outside, or the inside? I can't think in a hotel. There's nothing there to think about. At home, there are too many things to think about. In order to think properly, it is necessary to be neither here nor there. I don't have a hut but, if I stayed in the Heidegger room at the Library Hotel, might I be able to dwell there a while and, from there, be able to build on it?

    HEIDEGGER
    To give thought to homelessness is to
    take up residence within it.

To dwell is to intend to build, which means I can never quite dwell in the place where I live, at the same time I am living there.

Dwell has at least the intention of building concealed somewhere within it.

So does marriage.

I am trying to wind back time to find a moment we had a home we could dwell in but—dwell, sojourn—these are old-fashioned words. Who uses them anymore? I google *Xenia* but get photos of bikini'd models. Even on Stanford.edu, she's a pretty student, not a concept. Perhaps I expected too much of home. Perhaps I have no capacity to do any more than stay.

5 HOTEL DIARY

"In this homogeneous space series are broken and time abolished: a local pleasure is merely the ideal juxtaposition of its historical elements (delicious, luxurious, soft, thick) without their network of reciprocal determinations or their temporal intersection being involved. Luxury is perceived fundamentally in a space of projection without depth, of coincidence without development. There is only one plane and one moment."[1]

—MICHEL FOUCAULT, *THE BIRTH OF THE CLINIC*

```
Cast:
Sigmund Freud:        a psychoanalyst
Martin Heidegger:     a philosopher
Dora:                 a teenage girl
Mae West:             a sex symbol
The White Hotel:      a hotel
```

The lobby

Nowhere is more lonely; it's where I'm caught out first. I'm only one of many. It never feels right, that's the lobby problem. The doors let in the outside for just a moment. I cross a threshold from the hot street air that spills in. The women behind the desk wear shirts and jackets; the guests are in shorts, still sweating. At reception, I wait in one of the tub chairs that take up so little space because there is so little space here. In front of me the lifts come and go. I am excited to see who will come out of them: a thirty-something couple with apologetic shoulders both wearing preppy casual. To the hotel, they are a disappointment. But who could afford such luxury except those who have worked hard enough to care less about how they look. To the hotel, we are all disappointing. Everything is so beautiful, and so strange, how could we ever recognize ourselves here?

Lobby music blooms under our unlikely bodies, at no effort to the musicians, but at some effort to us, listening. It can still move us, stir our misshapen limbs, take hold of us coming back from the bar, drinks in hand, sway us helplessly; a song doesn't care how we look or when it will catch us again.

FREUD
Vorhof [vestibule], an anatomical term
for a particular region of the female
genitals.

In the lobby there is a sofa shaped like an enormous pair of lips.

It is called the Mae West sofa.

Surrealist artist Salvador Dalí was fascinated by movie actress Mae West's mouth. The original Mae West sofa measures 86.5 × 183 × 81.5 centimeters (34 × 72 × 32 inches) and was commissioned from Dalí by Edward James, a British patron of the arts with a particular interest in Surrealism. Surrealism was the art of dreams. In its first manifesto (1924), André Breton claimed that the movement would "resolve the previously contradictory conditions of dream and reality into an absolute reality, a super-reality."

```
             MAE WEST
  I only read biographies, metaphysics
  and psychology. I can dream up my own
  fiction.²
```

Herr K kissed Dora on the lips. Her father said she'd dreamed it up. Freud said she'd dreamed of it. Dora coughed, stopped breathing, suffered from sore throats, talked herself hoarse and finally, dried up.

Mae West was never a star of silent movies. Paramount offered her a contract in 1932 at the unusually advanced debut age of thirty-nine. She'd already made her name as a stage actress, and as the writer and producer of risqué vaudeville. Her first show was called "Sex." Sex was her appeal, but she was never exactly sexy, though she talked and wrote about sex, and she looked like sex. She was a sex symbol. And she wasn't exactly funny either, just funny peculiar. Her jokes are delivered flat, aggressive, knowing. What could have been funny understated is hammered home. Her jokes all sound like something you've heard before, something she's told six nights a week and twice on Saturdays. They sound like an acknowledgment of a joke, a repetition, an imitation. And that's what makes her wonderful. If her jokes had been funny, West would have been lame.

The lips sofa in the lobby is big, as big as Dalí's, but doesn't look exactly the same shape. Its texture is spongy. It gives. I sink entirely inside the mouth. I might be swallowed.

To maintain his personal comfort, Dalí licensed editions of his sofas but, now, imitations are unlimited. He also sold licenses for "monumental" and medium-size "museum versions" of sculptures based on his paintings, which had originally been no more than 2d. Due to the proliferation of unlicensed editions, and of copies, major auction houses are reluctant to sell Dalí sculptures. Most will recognize only those cited in Robert and Nicolas Descharnes' catalog, "The Hard and the Soft," although it is incomplete and increasingly out of date. As a result, some authentic pieces go unrecognized and imitations have sold at high prices.

Mae West's sassy, aggressive style had few, if any, imitators. There were even rumors that she was a female impersonator. After a number of successful pictures in the early 1930s, her career began to go west. In *Klondike Annie*, and then

Go West Young Man (both 1936), the Hays Movie Production Code made sure she shut her dirty mouth.

```
Linguistic usage follows the same
line in recognising the buttocks as
homologous to the cheeks, and by
drawing a parallel between the "labia"
and the lips.³
```

Even with their mouths shut, both Dora and West looked just like their bodies.

And that's what matters.

I sit gingerly on the Mae West sofa, in the teeth of some kind of uncertainty.

The library (which is also the lobby)

I have a friend who had a job creating libraries for hotel lobbies.

A library is not something usually found at home, but in a school, a university, or in a dedicated municipal building. The books in the library in this hotel do not matter. It only matters that the books are there. They are a holiday affair, and to read on holiday is so often to read lightly, though many of the books are thick and heavy. These are the casualties of old relationships, of flings between the sheets. Abandoned, only the first pages dog-eared, they show no evidence of commitment. The only glossies: the brochure for the hotel set open on the receptionist's desk, and brochures for other hotels, thickly funded by hotel ads so that, like the therapist's office, this hotel contains many other hotels. To step into the hotel lobby is to step not into one perfect hotel but into many. The effect is overwhelming.

HEIDEGGER

I am never here only.

What did he mean, Dr. H? That I can only visit a hotel I have previously imagined? He meant that we do not dwell in our environments. Our thoughts dwell also elsewhere. Our environments always allude to something else. This is style. Still, it is delightful to read of hotels from home, perhaps even (or especially) if a visit to a hotel is not in prospect. It is not, perhaps, so delightful to read of home from hotels, or of other hotels, from the hotel in which I am staying.

Dora dreamt that her father was dead. At home she, unconcerned, read from a thick book open on a desk, displayed like a hotel brochure in a lobby. Freud believed it was a dictionary.

FREUD

Dora had created for herself an
illness that she had read about in the

```
dictionary, and had punished herself
for reading it.
```

I have read of hotels and created a cure for myself in what I found there. Hotels are also written, don't think I don't know it: I have had a hand in writing them, not for these lobby brochures, but for others. I have written in an approved style, adding the odd tweak but unable to break the rubric. Hotels, I know, feed on their readers' presumed wish to have hotels presented in no other style than that of a hotel brochure—a performance of the performance I am not only witnessing but also participating in.

The switchboard

The switchboard is the link between the hotel and the not-hotel. But it is also the barrier.

Do hotels have switchboards anymore? They must. You can still call room to room, and press 9 for an outside line (which costs!). Now everyone has a mobile, there must be easier ways of being connected.

In her dictionary dream, Dora dreams she is at the train station going from, and to. She remembers either end of her journey. She does not remember the connections.

```
               FREUD
Ambiguous words are like switches or
points at a railway junction.
```

I can talk to you here in the hotel, and you will listen—not via the switchboard but the WiFi, that sometimes costs extra and sometimes does not—but I cannot talk to you about anything that matters. Outside the hotel I talk, but you do not listen, or I say things ambiguously, perhaps.

When I am in the hotel, you say things to me that I love. Sometime you ask me to come back. You can only ask me when I am away.

The stairs (The elevator)

I Going up

The stairs in the lobby are impressive and central.

Or, alternatively (in some small hotels) the lobby is under the stairs.

Everyone looks at the stairs, but most people use the elevators, which are hidden behind a screen, as though elevation were embarrassing.

Freud associated dreams of climbing stairs with the sensation of sexual exertion. At the time he treated Dora, Freud's clinic was upstairs from his home, which was in the apartment beneath.

I don't know if his building had an elevator.

DORA

(Describes her dream)

```
I see myself particularly clearly
going up the stairs.
```

(I have tripped up various hotel stairs, evaded reception, the parlor plants, the stair rods, the emergency lights, the fire extinguishers, laughed, been shushed, laid myself down on single beds, alone or accompanied . . . if not in body at least in mind: one man I kissed goodbye on the street invited me back to his hotel . . . and there were still others to whose hotels I would surely have gone, if only I had known where they were staying.)

```
     (Did) FREUD (say to DORA)
Will you come up sometime, and see
me?
```

(Where was Mrs. Freud all this time? One floor down, perhaps.)

DORA climbs the stairs to Freud's consulting room.

I climb the stairs to my hotel room.

II Going down

In another dream, Dora dreamt there was a fire at her house:

```
          DORA
We dash downstairs and, as soon as I'm
outside, I wake up.
```

When I go down in a lift, I get the same sensation in my stomach as when I'm coming.

Freud says nothing about sex and going downstairs.

In case of fire, the hotel notice warns me, do not take the elevator.

The corridor

Is next to everything is an inconvenience in which all doors are identical in which the floor which normally recedes dominates in which there is carpet on the walls sometimes the ceiling even in which there are no windows out of which it is difficult to get into somewhere else although this is its function in which elevator doors snap to and fire-escape fire doors are airtight in which each corridor on each floor is identical which has to provide maps and the floor number by the elevator to avoid confusion in which there are sometimes amenities which are also landmarks the ice machine the fire extinguisher the chip in the paintwork and (there used to be) the elevated ashtray.

The door (key)

When Dora stays by the lake, her father stays in a hotel but she stays in Herr K's home. She does not have a key. In Dora's home the dining room is locked. At home, Dora's brother is locked in his bedroom, which is on the other side of the dining room. At Dora's home, the larder is also locked, and Dora must ask her mother for the key. In Herr K's house nothing is locked. She does not have the key in Herr K's house, but instead of being unable to unlock, she is unable to lock. Herr K has the keys.

In my hotel, I have the key, but so does housekeeping. Someone can always get in when I am not around, or even when I am. Nevertheless, I lock the door at night. When I am home, but not with you, I lock the door, and put the chain across, which I do not do when you are there.

> DORA
> There might be a mishap during the
> night.

At home there are no internal locks. Why would there be?

> FREUD
> The case has opened smoothly to my
> collection of picklocks.[4]

I have lived in relation to desires, often other people's. It is easy to slot desire in. There is a hole in my side into which someone else's desires fit. It's only a matter of finding the right key, a key to the code, which is made of words. I must not want the key always to be a man.

No one who disdains the key can ever
unlock the door.

In the hotel, the key is a card. It looks just like a regular credit card and acts that way too. You slip it into the slot beside the door until the light goes green. The hotel reads the code, and you're in.

The bedroom

How soon do I unpack, admit this space is home?

There are so many things I could do here that I could also do at home, but I do not use the gadgets, which resemble, but are unlike, those I have at home: the flip-down ironing board, the trouser press, the hairdryer on its long air-duct tube that will only work with the pressure of a cocked thumb, the mini-bar. These things set me against the hotel authorities. I could put my own champagne in the fridge, but it wouldn't fit. Everything reminds me: the hotel is not on my side, not really.

The hotel suspects even me of wanting to steal its coat hangers (quite rightly). The hangers are rings threaded onto a steel bar, with wooden shoulders hooked on below. Oh they are strange, like people who lose their heads, who fall apart too easy. What would be the use of them, outside this place? They all have a screw loose.

I thread my clothes on, obedient.

My dress hangs alone in the wardrobe, the shape of a woman with no one inside, no head, no legs. Even if it had legs its feet wouldn't touch the floor. I take it down. I wake up, my clothes on the floor, or tangled in the sheets' whiteness. Wear colored underwear; it'll be easier to find after. Whatever the decor, the sheets are always the color of erasure.

Some hotels are decorated entirely in white. I stayed in one once, in a white city. It was a white box.

THE WHITE HOTEL
The white room is dedicated to a sense
of well being, providing fresh white
products. The terrasse concepts have a
private roof-top outdoor terrace with
its own jacuzzi.

In the white hotel I stay in a room on an upper floor. It is square, and everything in it is white. The square bed is high, like a bed in a hospital, high enough to need square block steps leading up to it.

The square French doors lead out onto a small right-angled balcony. The room also has smaller, square, double-glazed windows that don't open. The microwaved supper arrives in a square white bowl.

THE WHITE HOTEL
The room is white hence the name of

the concept. The bed looks like a
table. The bathtub looks like a canopy
with a plexiglas "bath sky dome."

Below in the courtyard, square white umbrellas.
Because the sun gets very white here too.
The white hides the hotel's sharp corners.

FREUD
The two families had rented a floor
in the hotel together, and one day
Frau K had announced that she could
not keep the bedroom which she been
sharing up to that point with one of
her children, and a few days later
Dora's father gave up his bedroom and
they both moved into new rooms, the
end rooms which were separated only by
the corridor.

At one time Dora had slept in Frau K's bedroom.
Frau K is white. Frau K is ideal. Except she is not.
Frau K is not liked by her husband.
Frau K is liked by Dora's father.

HERR K
You know I get nothing from my wife.

DORA'S FATHER
I get nothing out of my own wife.

Dora's father gives Frau K something. He gives Dora, Frau K, and his wife jewelry that is alike, but he does not like white jewelry. He does not like his wife's pearls. He substitutes a bracelet.

DORA

Mama . . . got a lot of it from papa.

Herr K likes Dora.
    Herr K, says Freud, is like Dora's father.
    Dora, says Freud, thinks Freud is like Herr K.
    Dora is nothing like her mother, so she says.
    (Freud never doubts her on this one.)
    Dora's father is impotent.
    Frau K asks her husband to give her nothing.
    Nothing happens in Frau K.
    Dora thinks she is ideal.

THE WHITE HOTEL

The room becomes a structure for welcoming micro-events in relation to the concept of space. In this way, comfort goes beyond mere physical or visual comfort. This is comfort at work, produced by the generosity and simplicity of the structures which, like operating instructions, invite us to take advantage of the present moment. These spaces are based

on an openness of volumes, a non-
specialisation of structures. This has
the effect of smoothing the transition
from one activity to another and of
sharing one's [sic] experiences.

Sic.
    All sic.
    Where is marriage?
    In what white room furnished.
    Where were the white flowers?
    With its own presents.
    Does the hotel stay in us?
    Can I cure myself of home here?

Dreamwork

I came to the hotel with a kind of tiredness I can't sleep away.
Is it from being on these toes, tipped forward all day in hotel
heels? When I am asleep, I am still paying (or working) for
my hotel though I am not making the most of it. Or perhaps
I am.

FREUD
Every dream is a desire represented
as fulfilled. . . . Only unconscious
desires, or those that extend into the

unconscious, have the power to form a
dream.

I don't remember any of the dreams I've had in hotels.

The en-suite

Is all angles, and the angles reflect, white: the tiles, the corner
of the shower head, unexpected. Me?
Yes you are, but what am I?
In the mirror, I don't see myself, perhaps because I'm
not at home here. In the en-suite of a railway compartment,
Freud failed to recognize himself.

> FREUD
> A more than usually violent jolt of
> the train swung back the door of the
> adjoining washing-cabinet, and an
> elderly gentleman in a dressing gown
> and a travelling cap came in.[5]

It was himself of course. But Freud didn't want to travel in a
train that would have someone like him for a member.
(Wait—was that a Freudian slip?)

> FREUD
> One need only turn each individual

reproach back on the person of the
speaker.

Edward James, the patron of Dalí's Mae West sofa, also commissioned Magritte's painting *Not to be Reproduced* in which we see a man's suit-clad torso from behind. He looks into a mirror, which, instead of reflecting his face, shows the back of his own head repeated. Although the subject has no recognizable features, it is said to be a portrait of James.

Herr K, Frau K, Dora, Dora's Mother, Dora's Father, Freud look into their mirrors. They see each other. It is impossible for them to recognize themselves as they are seen by any of the others.

Wife or mother, daughter or lover, father or teenager: each can be substituted for several of the others. That's why *A Fragment* never ends.

(En-Suite, because "in-room toilet" sounds anything but glamorous.

Suite means "next."

So, next.)

The restaurant

I The bar

Is, like the lobby, a link to the outside. You can enter it from the street door, or from the hotel.

Is a place to see and be seen, which is difficult: it is almost impossible to do something, and, at the same time, see yourself doing it.

De 5 à 7 (or from 6 to 8, or whatever), waiting, I am at home. I'm waiting, because I have the waiting habit. Commuters are lucky—their time taken up by from and to. Even if they don't remember the connections, their waiting, at least, is moving. At home, at this time I'd be waiting to make the food, waiting while making the food, waiting for people to eat it, unable to leave, to do anything else, in case they arrive. Too early to drink (though I will); too late to get started on anything. In the hotel restaurant, over the stoned olives' little assholes, I will put myself *at the mercy.*

This is not the same kind of waiting as at home, as the waiter, eventually, and not even after a very long pause, arrives.

I wait to be waited on. A double pleasure.

Not so much to feel cared for as to be seen to be cared for. See. .? Feel. .?

I can only fall in love bypassing the waiter. But, already anticipating my desires, he is everywhere.

II The restaurant

Since I left home, I've been a hotel ghost, living on chocolates, coffee, dregs of champagne and candle ends. There's no longer such a thing as lunch, or dinner, only a series of atomized teatimes and cocktail hours, tiny meals (it is not so easy to be hungry in the midst of plenty).

The older people sat in the restaurant and the younger people sat in the bar, not that they were so very young, the men still dressed in hoodies, and the women smarter and not eating bread because they'd heard somewhere some movie star didn't and, although they didn't of course believe that they themselves were movie stars or even potential movie stars, they might have believed themselves to be on some kind of parallel track, perhaps in the story of a movie. They made me nervous. Imitating them, I didn't order a starter, then regretted it. People are uglier when there are a lot of them together.

Why are hotel restaurants almost always disappointing? Salty, beefy, sweet, brittle.

Well, hunger meets what meets it.

How women eat together. You see everything: the private in public, the pressing of things on each other, the forced-sharing; I'll have one of those, but only if no one else wants it. I'll order one if you'll have some. They order the sourdough with tough crusts. They order toast with nothing, one egg between them. They have had a lifetime behind them of taking leftovers. It is no fun dining with other women, only with men who will order the T-bone, who will graciously share their fries. "It's nice toast though," the women say, "it's a nice cup of tea."

The women are wearing dresses, mostly, which shows that they are here to enjoy the food, or to enjoy their enjoyment of each other eating the food, which is something that can be eaten up by the eye.

Or maybe they wear the dresses for work.

The woman sitting at the table across the room is so pretty. And to notice that, additionally, she has an inner life, however carefully she hides it from the man sitting opposite. She does not show it very often. But she will show it here, to you, now. There are other women, but they are carefully hiding their inner lives—they'd not like to show to just anyone—and no one notices. But here is one who has. And yet she looks so pretty too. And later, when she is older, she will be all inner life and no outer, not that anyone would notice her then. But right now her inner life is all yours. But without the outer, who would bother? Without the pretty case she is nothing but an unshelled snail: soft and ugly, not even nice to eat. How delightful! Your discovery. Women who look like that, you have been taught, have no inner life. Yet here is one who both looks and lives, though she will not show both to many, not to many who will notice. Only to you.

She leaves, he leaves. Three females left, each sitting alone. We do not cohere because women in a restaurant are nothing cohesive. We slide off one another, between us no solidarity. A woman alone must be compared to other women. A woman alone is dangerous. Without context she is ageless (or maybe only less aged). Completed neither by other women nor by children, she is an invitation to completion by a man.

(Or maybe her incompleteness is magnificent.)

There are no men here eating alone, though there are men eating together, in twos, threes, fours, wearing business suits so we can tell they are not here strictly for pleasure. The men without business suits are eating with women, who take their pleasure for them. A hotel is no place for a man without a business suit to take pleasure, alone.

I like to see a man eating well, so well that he could almost take over that function for me. They get so hungry, and the food is absorbed so quickly into their square bodies that in me would produce nothing more than spare rounds of flesh. Men are so content to be helpless. My husband can't operate the coffee machine, my father cannot cook a meal, has no idea what goes into the food he likes. They are content not to know the most basic ways of servicing their bodies.

Perhaps these men are different.

What is there to do in a hotel restaurant, alone, but watch other people? I find myself never a woman—never at any point. Then I hear of women being spoken of and look, and there they are. I see them, just as men do. I see men employing them, loving them, buying them glasses of wine from the bar. But when I look back, it's like a trick of the light. From where I sit, I see no women, just this person, and that person.

I do not go into

The Swimming pool; the billiards room; the gym, the club. Someone once told me the rich are not afraid to use anything. But perhaps hotels are not for the *really* rich. . . . Is a hotel an inconvenience, in the end?

6 IN A GERMAN PENSION

Do you suppose that now you have finally lighted your bonfire you are going to find it a peaceful and pleasant thing—you are going to prevent the whole house from burning?

—KATHERINE MANSFIELD, *IN A GERMAN PENSION*

```
Cast:
Dora:                    a teenage girl
Freud:                   a psychoanalyst
Herr Rat:                a guest
Mae West:                a sex symbol
Katherine Mansfield:     a writer
KM:                      her avatar
```

I

When they could no longer stand it, or themselves, Freud's clients went to a hotel. And when a hotel no longer met their needs, they moved to a spa and, from there, to a sanatorium.

A hotel already knows there is something wrong with you. A spa hotel is a melancholy place catering to ordinary unhappiness, sanctioning the desires it treats. A sanatorium is a clinic, but is also luxurious. I'm not sure when a spa hotel becomes a sanatorium.

I have been ill several times in hotels, as though I chose to go there not to recover, but to be sick, to get rid of something, to have my illness out of the way of other people, and their interference. That way, I have kept well and sane a good deal of the time. What good did it do me? I don't know. I only knew that not to be this way could have hurt others obscurely in ways they might not themselves have understood.

-Doctor, doctor, I think there's something wrong with me.
(No, I meant to say I feel there's something wrong with me.)
-Where do you feel it?
(The patient is always the straight man.)
-In lots of different places. What do you advise?
-Well, I advise you not to visit any of those places again.

Some aches become me. It becomes difficult not to sustain them. When I am sick, putting on clothes feels fake. Washing my body is washing something belonging to someone else. Where should my illness take place? I can hardly imagine an out-of-body experience, wouldn't know where else to go.

I could seek asylum in a hotel to get away from it all (as if I ever could), but there are diseases that strike you in hospitals, diseases, perhaps, *of* hospitals.

To be in a hotel is to have a complaint, or to feel the tension of being about to complain, or to have the possibility of complaining, which is not possible at home. It is difficult to find a hotel for an angry woman but, at home, who would she complain to? If you have a complaint at home, you keep it to yourself, more shame you. You lie on your bed, and then you have to make it. Every day.

From what do I wish to be cured?

I must find something.

I want my temperature taken hourly, my pillow smoothed, my corners hospitalized. I want cool water and a straw, I want to be referred for treatment. I want to be referred to in the first person plural. I want to begin to refer to myself in the third person singular. I want my body parts to have personalities, as though I were in charge of an unruly playground. I want them to be disciplined. I want to be gently smothered by authority, all for the good of my health, to eat strange things at regular times, to be weighed and not to measure up. I want it to be time for something to be done about me; it's too late for me to do anything for myself. I want to be told to do things, then told to do nothing. I want to be put into unfamiliar machines. I want the machines to do something for me. I want hydrotherapy, psychotherapy, physiotherapy. I want it all to hurt, *just a little* more than they say. I want to be nursed (oh yes!), I want to be gently, but firmly, physically humiliated. I want to be a hopeless case. I want them to say there's hope; I want to be out of danger, I want to be brought back from the dead. I want life support. I want my body and my mind to be preserved by "hypocritic" oath. I want to be the stain on the bathroom tiles. If I am here to be ill, I will be. I am here to lack something, to uncomplete myself. I want to convalesce but never leave, because everything outside the hotel is sick.

The reality is, I get sick in hotels. But what I'm sick of isn't hotels.

I used to call it hypochondria.

I didn't want to call it anything else.

I blocked it with the name, perhaps. Words can do that. Some words are cul-de-sacs: they prevent anything enacting off the page. They're just as good as aphonia.

II

A proper disease involves distance, and systems: trains, police, border controls, quarantine, passports, room numbers, bank-card numbers, and somewhere to locate it.

(*You never go on holiday where you live.*)

Dora's dad was taken out of the family to be cured. His cure was physical: it was located in a spa. Dora's cure was mental. It was presumed to be located in a psychologist's office.

When Dora, or her father, are ill, they go away from home, where they recover. When they return they slowly become ill again. Diseases are not always caught in the street. Sometimes they're familial. "He was sick before the marriage," said Dora's aunt. Perhaps she means syphilis, a family disease that Dora's feared her dad had passed on to her, as well as to his wife. It was a disease that did not come from home, neither from his childhood home, nor from the one he made with Dora and her mother. It might have been caught in a hotel. In any case, it took up residence in Dora's home, and made it necessary for Dora, her father—and, sometimes, her mother—to leave home, to search for a cure.

(Even Dora's mother must be cured of home sometimes.)

So Dora leaves for a spa, but she travels there not with her mother, but her father. Dora's mother already isn't there. Throughout *A Fragment*, she is away (which is, in her case, at home). She is like Cinderella's mother, like Snow White's mother, like Bambi's mother, like the mother of The Little Mermaid. These mothers are not needed in those stories, or it seems that their absence is needed. As "Dora" is not a story but a (case) history, Dora's mother cannot, like them, be killed for the sake of the plot. But she is near absent from Freud's analysis.

FREUD

The story of a mother's love usually
becomes a model for the daughter.

But Freud does not tell us the story of Dora's mother's love.

I never met her mother.

Like Dora, like her father, and her mother, I sought the cure away from home, where the cause resided.

I do not know the story of my mother's love. Perhaps I do not want to know it.

III

In 1909, Katherine Mansfield, a writer from New Zealand, arrived at a German hotel that adjoined a spa. Like its other inhabitants, she was there for a cure. From this visit came her first book of stories, *In A German Pension*.

The German Pension in the book is a "family hotel," but it does not contain entire families. Every family is missing a member (usually the male member who, somehow, seldom needed to be cured). A family hotel can also refer to the family that runs it, not the family that stays there, the family that will provide a family atmosphere, which is so very unlike your own family, and who will adopt you, temporarily, into theirs, without any of your family's inconveniences. Their son tends the bar; their daughter waits tables. The whole family is there to serve you.

To show the family away from home is to show it at its most powerful. That it exists outside its setting without splitting, crumbling, is to show something almost invincible. To become invincible it must harden. You see them sometimes, in hotel restaurants: parents and children with adjoining rooms; across the tables, faces that, over the years, have practiced love upon one another. A small family hotel was always the sort I could never afford. In a hotel the economics of family are laid bare. Only the rich stay in hotels as families, can afford to take members who cannot pay for themselves. Being rich enough to stay with each other, they find they have nowhere else to go.

I did not review family hotels.

It is a luxury not to think about family.

In the German Pension, all they can talk about is home.

"Germany," the traveler boomed, "is the home of the family."

"What is your husband's favourite meat?" asked the widow. Katherine Mansfield's narrator (avatar?—she is unnamed: let's call her KM) cannot say. The widow says "You would not have kept house, as his wife, for a week without knowing that fact."

Marriage is not what it contains, but its structure. It is not the nature of promises given; it is its bond. The contents of its bond are not set. They are no more than a set of family resemblances.

Does anything resemble a family?

Herr Rat likes to stay in family hotels without families.

HERR RAT
I have had all I wanted from women,
without marriage.

Katherine Mansfield was married.

Herr K was married.

Frau K was married.

Dora's dad was married.

None of them, it seems, to what they desired.

Desire was what took place outside marriage.

On the other hand:

Freud was married.

Dora was not married.

KM was not married.

Mae West was married, but she didn't want anyone to know. She kept her marriage a secret. It wouldn't do to tell what she desired. She and he made a home together, she said, "only for several weeks."[1]

```
               MAE WEST
  Marriage  is  a  great  institution,  but
  I'm not ready for an institution.[2]
```

No one in *A Fragment* questions that desire is not desirable. I am hardly surprised. A hotel is an institution in which there is nothing I could not be trained to desire.

IV

At the German Pension, KM's enemies are often married—"successful businessmen," and their wives, heavy as suitcases.

Open them up and, inside, you'd find: offal, bread soup, sauerkraut, boys' boots, cherry cake with cream, whalebone stays, hemorrhoids, and a little unattended dusty regret. Inside, the men, and the women are just the same. But "marriage certainly changed a woman more than it did a man," says one of them, who keeps a photograph of his wife, single: "She doesn't look like my wife—like the mother of my son."

KM

I consider child-bearing the most
ignominious of professions.

"Now I have had nine children and they are all alive, thank God," says the fat German Pension guest.

In the German Pension, marriage ends in childbed—something to be frightened of for physical and mental reasons. Each child brings a portion of suffering, even unproblematic children, and this suffering must be distributed, fairly or unfairly (always, in Mansfield's stories, unfairly). Pregnant women and mothers come to the spa by the German Pension. Their condition is a peculiar kind of illness.

FREUD

Once the child has become a woman
and, in contradiction of the demands
of her childhood, has married an
inattentive man who suppresses her

```
will, unstintingly exploits her work
and expends neither affection nor
money upon her, illness becomes the
only weapon with which she can assert
herself in life. It gives her the
rest she craves. It forces the man to
make sacrifices of money and care that
he wouldn't have made to the healthy
woman.
```

The cure in the German Pension does not seem to work. Many of the guests return every year, leaving their marriages behind. What is it they want to be cured from?

V

Katherine Mansfield, like KM, her avatar, was pregnant by a man who was not her husband (her marriage was one of hasty convenience). Being with child, but not part of a family, her mother sent her to a spa hotel.

"With" child. Such a good, ambiguous phrase: with. Not dwelling, only staying a while. But no one gives birth in hotels. Or do they?

```
                   MOM
We walked in and I am telling you I
was like, I am having this baby here.
It was gorgeous.³
```

"Every woman deserves a birth like this," said the journalist, a birth away from home, where there is no home work. "All of our crap isn't there. There is no pile of bills on the desk. The dirty dishes aren't in the sink. The laundry basket isn't right there filled with towels we need to put away." In the hotel where the mom gave birth, there are "Superior Accommodations," there are "Deluxe Accommodations," and there are "Club Accommodations." Then it's suite. It's impossible to start any lower. The decor of the hotel is "both nostalgic and modern. A 42-inch HDTV, DVD player, MP3 port and complimentary Wi-Fi, fulfil your entertainment needs." The velvet couch is "expertly placed," and the room is "grounded only by chocolate carpeting." In its largest suite, "One and a half baths ensures convenience while entertaining." The Club Level is "100% smoke free."

                    FREUD
There's no fire without smoke.

(Or did I get that wrong?)

Katherine Mansfield was pregnant in her German Pension, until she slipped while miscarrying a heavy suitcase, which she was trying to put on top of a wardrobe.

(I am not pregnant.)

Dora was not pregnant, but nine months after Herr K kissed her, Dora gave birth to appendicitis. Then to a limp. Katherine Mansfield gave birth to . . . nothing.

A magic trick—there was nothing inside the box.

KM (Mansfield's narrator/avatar) is unmarried but, when asked, discovers it is possible to give birth to a phantom husband (a sea captain, of all things). What a feat of ratiocination!

In the comments box beneath the hotel birth article: "I would rather stay in a hotel room that a baby had been born in, than a room where someone had a hooker!"

In the comments box beneath another article about the birth: "Maybe I'm wrong, but I don't think that's fair for the next hotel guest."[4]

Whoever thinks about the next hotel guest?

Dora's mother might have. She, says Freud, cleans the house so as not to be dirty.

FREUD

```
Her genitals, which ought to
have been kept clean, had been
dirtied . . . [Dora] seems to
understand that her mother's mania for
cleanliness was a reaction against
this dirtying.[5]
```

Dora, a scholar, scorns home work, but she also does not want to be dirty.

That's the problem, isn't it, and it's the same problem now.

Who will clean the house?

Who will be dirty?

A cook in the kitchen, a lady in the living room, a whore...

Should I be one, or the other? Could I be all three? Is there a way to avoid being any of them?

All these problems are solved in hotels.

VI

FREUD
A Freudian slip is where you say one
thing, but mean your mother.

Freud did not say that. It's a joke (and, like many jokes, is anon).

It is a joke about parapraxis, in which the speaker expresses an unconscious wish, hidden inside a box of words that both reveal and conceal it. A parapraxis sounds like a joke, but it is an unintentional one. Freud did not name it the Freudian slip. He called these speech patterns *Fehlleistungen*, which means faulty actions. Sometimes, when they cannot be spoken, words enact off the page.

FREUD
If one's lips are silent, one will be
voluble with one's fingertips, betrayal
seeps through every pore.

Dora fiddles with her handbag.

> FREUD
> She was wearing a little purse around
> her neck, in a style that was modern
> at the time, and she played with it.

> DORA
> Why shouldn't I wear a little bag
> like this, when it happens to be in
> fashion?

> FREUD
> The little bag, like the jewellery
> box, once again representative of the
> Venus shell, the female genitalia!

> DORA
> I knew you'd say that.

A symptom is a kind of *Fehlleistungen*. It is the physical evidence of something unspeakable.

> FREUD
> A symptom is a sign of, and a
> substitute for, an instinctual
> satisfaction which has remained in
> abeyance.[6]

A symptom is an action that, like a word, stands in for a something else, but it is not like a regular word that stands in directly, but more like one of these word forms, that are a bit like Freudian slips, and jokes, as they suggest two things at the same time.

FREUD

```
(Symptoms are)
Like garlands of flowers stretched over
metal wire.
```

(This is simile.)

FREUD

```
Since bed and board constitute
marriage.⁷
```

(This is metonymy.)

FREUD

```
[A symptom is]
The grain of sand around which the
mollusc forms the pearl.
```

(This is metaphor.)

My bed stands in the middle of my hotel room. Important, would you say, sacrificial, would you say, ceremonial? No. Mansfield (or her avatar) despised metaphor, metonymy: "My dear little lady," says Herr Erchardt, "you must not take the quotation literally."

KM's narrator refuses abstraction, but she also despises her own solid legs, the German Pension's solid food, the solid bodies of the Germans and their children, and their bodily functions, which so delight them, especially when they turn them into words.

KM worries about bodies. Her physical condition produces mental symptoms (disgust).

Dora's neuroses enact physically (Freud says, "somatically").

A somatic symptom, says Freud, is neuroses' "escape route into the physical."

Dora is a physical case.

KM is a mental case.

I am always escaping. I am no more than a suitcase.

VII

I think of a dream as something like a hotel wardrobe. It has an inside and an outside. It is waiting to be filled. But two feet do not seem enough to support such a massy piece of furniture. A suitcase stands upon two wheels and is, perhaps, a more suitable metaphor.

My suitcase stands in the corner of my hotel room, small and black, square-shouldered as a visiting psychoanalyst.

It clasps its hands behind its back and says *tell me about your symptoms*.

No, I will tell it about Dora's dream.

Dora dreamt that her house will burn down. Her mother wanted to save her jewelry; her father became angry and insisted the family must escape without it. In any case, Dora's father did not like Dora's mother's jewelry.

DORA

Mama and Papa had a big row about a piece of jewellery. Mama wanted to wear something particular, drop pearls in her ears. But Papa doesn't like that kind of thing, so instead of the drop pearls he brought her a bracelet. She was furious, and told him that if he'd spent so much money on a present that she didn't like then he should give it to someone else.

FREUD
(To Dora)

So far you've talked about the jewellery and said nothing about a box.

> DORA
> (Says nothing about the box)

> FREUD
> You may not know that "Jewellery box"
> is a popular expression used to refer
> to something you recently alluded to
> when you talked about the handbag,
> that is, the female genitals.

It never does to explain a joke, but that's psychoanalysis, I guess.

> FREUD
> I give both organs and processes their
> technical names. . . . I call a spade
> a spade.

There are no spades in my hotel, no evidence of home work, or any other kind of work, only of its results. And indeed Freud did not say, "I call a spade a spade," as it appears in the English translation of *A Fragment*, but "j'appelle une chat une chat" (I call a cat a cat).

> FREUD
> One can talk to girls and women about
> all kinds of sexual matters without
> doing them any harm.

Freud denies that mentioning a spade produces the frisson that calls the spade into action.

A spade is made for action but a symptom is the product of inaction, of "an instinctual satisfaction which has remained in abeyance." It acts, but not like a spade. It is impossible for a spade to act in a hotel.

FREUD

No one can undertake the treatment of a case of hysteria until he is convinced of the impossibility of avoiding the mention of sexual subjects.

Or, as Freud says (again, in French), "You can't make an omelette without breaking eggs."

You could break an egg with a spade, but it might not make for a good omelette.

You could make an omelette for a cat, but it might not lay eggs.

Freud calls a symptom a "conversion disorder." It is true; my house is in disorder. I want something to happen, some kind of conversion. When I return from the hotel I must make myself a better house. I must convert it into what? A home? Would it have helped if I had at least spoken about things differently, if I could, perhaps, have itemized what went into home, described even the things I could not see:

the gutter round the roof, the tiles? If I had been able to put home into different sorts of words?

When I see a spade, I'll call it a cat.

When I see a cat, I'll call it an egg.

As Freud wrote to his friend Arnold Zweig: "I, as is well known, do not like cats."[8]

As soon as I see anything, I'll break it.

```
            DENISE RILEY
There is a lonely hour which never
quite arrives, of the nonmetaphoricity
of language.⁹
```

Maybe it is a place, not an hour, or maybe it's a time and a place. A hotel, with a window, but also a lace curtain, or a double-glazed pane, that darkens in response to light from outside. Something indirect, a metaphor, a slip of the tongue says Freud, can be direct as nothing else is.

VIII

Dora's Case of Hysteria is also her mother's case, which is a jewel case.

Like Dora, I do not wear jewels, and do not have a jewel case with me, but I have my suitcase. In it I keep my clothes. They are important to me. I have been told that they become me and, in them, I have always the option of being transported. You do not give me jewelry. You want to, you say, but, unlike Dora's father, you say I must choose. If you choose, you say, I may not like it. I want you to choose, I say, because if I choose, it is not a gift. One day, as Herr K to Dora, you give me a jewelry box. You chose it. I try to disguise that I think it is ugly. Some years later you tell me you think it's ugly too.

I am still using it.

I pack my suitcase, with its two wheels and a pullout handle, with so few things, that they barely cover one half of its empty shell. It shuts like an oyster. When I turn a corner, it hops on one wheel.

Here is its other foot.

For several years before I reached the age of ten I kept a bag under my bed containing my most treasured possessions so that I could escape in case of fire. I can't remember for how many years this went on, but it meant that I seldom used my most treasured possessions. The bag did contain a money box, though not a jewelry box. My money box was beautifully made: wooden, in the form of a dice. Its sides slid open in a secret combination of moves. I still have it, though it is broken.

"There was never a real fire at our house," said Dora.

Because I was always ready for escape, the fire in my house never happened.

IX

At first the symptom is the unwelcome
guest of the psychical life.

What if I went from cause to cure, without manifesting any
symptom, direct from the situation of illness to the situation
of cure, from home to hotel? A hotel looks like an escape
route, but Freud tells me there's always something inside
something else. Just as a guest must fit the desires the hotel
offers to satisfy, so symptoms are broken down into a series
of recognizable categories: a room for each guest, a symptom
for each neurosis, or sometimes, as in a hotel, for several.
Freud also says the symptom can remain after the cause is
lost, that the symptom can become its own cause, hollowed
out. To seek a cure is a symptom, perhaps. To stay in a hotel
is, itself, a symptom.

FREUD

The practical goal of the treatment
lies in the abolition of all possible
symptoms.

What am I being cured from anyway? I've forgotten. You can
go to hotels to be cured long after you know your disease.

A hotel produces its own symptoms.
If I lose my symptoms, I may disappear.
They are eggshells of desire.

7 HOTEL MARX (BROS.)

"You don't have to be mad to work here, but it helps."

(ANONYMOUS)

```
Cast:
Wilde:                a playwright
English person:       a registrar
New Zealander:        a patient
Leo:                  a playwright
Groucho:              an entrepreneur
Repo Man:             a repo man
Margaret Dumont:      a straight woman
Chico:                a Marx Bro.
Hotel Inspector:      a hotel inspector
Woman:                a love interest
Harpo:                a-phonic
```

When they could no longer stand it, or themselves, Freud's clients went to a hotel. And when a hotel no longer met their needs, they moved to a spa, then to sanatorium, where, sometimes, they would die.

The first hospitals were little different from almshouses. Hospitals were for the poor, who could not be treated at home, whose ailments excluded them from home. Hotels, whose treats cannot be given at home, are for the rich—both are bound to their clients by cash, or lack of it.

```
        OSACR WILDE
        (In a hotel)
  I am dying beyond my means.
```

The first hospitals' guests also lacked social capital—children, the sick, the elderly, those who could not do home work— and also those who would not, whose refusal made them indecent: prostitutes, unmarried mothers, the homeless, the disabled, the unacceptable, and those whose mental symptoms would now be treated in a clinic. The poor were more likely to be indecent, and the indecent were more likely to be hidden in hospitals. Even the unhomely must find a home somewhere.

Oscar Wilde was arrested at a hotel in London, for "gross indecency." At his trial he was forced to defend the decency of his writing, which was brought in evidence against him. Sometimes words enact off the page. Sometime later, Wilde died in a hotel in Paris, right across the river from God's hotel—The Hotel Dieu—which is a hospital. A hospital (in premedical times, when it was also an almshouse) used to be more like a hospice. It was for terminal decline. A cure was not expected. It was an overnight stop between this world and the next, where no one lived for long.

Let's decline:

To be hospitable.

To be hostile.

To be hospital.

To be hospice.

Now there are even hotels in hospitals,[1] so the well can stay alongside the sick, though in different quarters now disease is no longer familiar, but a private matter (common factors: the possibilities of service, cleanliness, ghosts, death, authority, hospitality, and being thrown out). Both guests and patients are given over to the care of strangers. I worked in a hospice for a while. It was white, mostly. Some patients like to decorate their rooms, I was told; others leave them blank: white walls, white sheets. Some people prefer to make an end only in somewhere that looks a hotel.

I have also stayed in the hotel where Oscar Wilde died, but not in his room. The wallpaper in the Wilde Room, which I did not see, is not white, but richly colored and patterned. I stayed in another room that overlooked the back of the hotel.

```
                    WILDE
                   (Dying)
    Either this wallpaper goes, or I do.
```

This is a misquote. He really said, "The wallpaper and I are fighting a duel to the death. One or the other of us has to go."[2] This is not parapraxis but elision. Time's elided too: I have read that Wilde said this several weeks before he died. Still, it is a joke and, like a hospital, and a hotel, a joke draws attention to the fact that it contains something that also remains hidden.

ENGLISH REGISTRAR
Did you come here to die?

NEW ZEALAND PATIENT
(Perhaps KM)
No, I came here yester-die.

Perhaps it was not a registrar, but a receptionist; perhaps the patient mistook the hospital for a hotel. It's easy enough: many jokes take place in hotels; most involve a misunderstanding between the server and the served. Well I guess it serves them both right. This joke triangulates on our knowing how British and New Zealand English enact off the page. Most puns depend on a familiarity with the unfamiliar. Many jokes involve strangers. Most jokes deal with anxiety that, Freud said, is the reenactment of the memory of an approaching terror. No one likes to speak of death, especially in a hospital, or a hotel.

I

In *Room Service* (1938), the Marx Bros. are living at a hotel. They are theater producers. They cannot pay their bill, and they are waiting for a visit from a backer, who will bring a check. They want to continue to stay in the hotel but are afraid of being caught out by the hotel manager, who is being watched by the hotel inspector, who, he says, is being surveyed by his company from which he hopes for promotion. Dora is surveyed severally—by her father, Herr K, and Freud, who recounts their accounts. Dora's mother and Frau K do not surveil her, or this surveillance is not reported by Freud.

In order to remain in the hotel, the Marx Bros. must appear to be ill or, rather, Leo (Frank Albertson), the writer of their play, must appear to develop symptoms. They paint spots on Leo's face. He has a tapeworm, they tell the hotel manager, and laryngitis. Like Dora, he cannot speak. Then he really becomes sick. It's difficult to tell *somata* from genuine illness.

The symptoms are produced by the producers' lack of money (in the Marx Bros.' movies someone is always going bankrupt).

> LEO
> Say what kind of a hotel is this? You move in and you owe $600 right away.

Someone knocks at the Marx Bros.' hotel room door:

> GROUCHO
> Shh . . . money!

They are expecting their theater backer's agent, but it is the
REPO MAN trying to claim a payment on Leo's typewriter.

> GROUCHO
> He tore up all his money.

> REPO MAN
> He must be out of his mind . . .
> Where did they take him?

> GROUCHO
> The maternity hospital.

> REPO MAN
> The maternity hospital? But I thought
> you said he was crazy.

> GROUCHO
> Well if he wasn't crazy, he wouldn't
> go to the maternity hospital.

There are no mothers in the plot of *Room Service*, no
Margaret Dumont to chase Groucho, as she does in seven of
the other Marx Bros. movies, just two young women, who do
not pursue anyone, but who are both love interests.

> WILDE
> All women become like their mothers,
> that is their tragedy.

The two women in the play are one-man women, and the men are one-woman men. No one is exchangeable for anyone else and there are not enough women to go around. In *Room Service* there are no girls for Harpo to chase, as there are in other Marx Bros. movies, though the movie poster shows him chasing a miniskirted chambermaid. Instead he watches the lovers in the park. As he must stay in the hotel, and all the women in the hotel are spoken for, he must watch them through the hotel window, as if they were a silent film.

(*Dora avoids watching lovers in the street. They disgust her.*)

The theater backer will fund the Marx Bros.' play, he says, if they will give a part to his girlfriend, but there is no part for her. As in *Room Service* itself, most of the cast of Leo's play is male.

> GROUCHO
> The young lady can play one of the miners.

(Is there a joke about minors here? Dora was fourteen when Herr K first kissed her.)

> LEO
> But the miners are all men!

> GROUCHO
> Do me a favour and keep sex out of this conversation.

```
I've never produced anything but clean
plays!
```

GROUCHO claimed his female straight man, Dumont, was his most successful foil because she never understood what was indecent about his jokes.

```
        MARGARET DUMONT:
There is an art to playing the
straight role. You must build up your
man but never top him, never steal the
laughs.³
```

Because she is not there, hearing innocently, because there is no Dumont, the mother/lover, the feminine at its most terrifying, there is little opportunity, in *Room Service*, for indecency. *Room Service* is a cleaned-up version of a Marx Bros. movie—the movie was not written by the Marx Bros. but was originally a Broadway play first produced in 1937.

The Marx Bros. worry about a visit from "the hotel dick."

"Are you the hotel dick?" they ask everyone.

The hotel dick turns out, after all, to be the hotel doctor.

The doctor is repeatedly mistaken for the hotel dick, by different characters. That's transference perhaps.

Everyone is expecting the hotel dick, but, like KM's husband, he never comes.

II

Later in the movie, the Marx Bros. again cannot pay their bill. This time the hotel manager incarcerates them in the hotel until they can pay. The room they wanted to get into has become the room they want to get out of.

> CHICO
> Let's let off the fire alarm!

> GROUCHO
> It ain't a fire alarm without a fire.

HARPO gestures (Harpo, like Dora, has aphonia).

> CHICO
> (always Harpo's interpreter)
> Alrighta then let's have a fire.

(Dora dreams there is a fire, and that her mother wants to save her jewelry box.)

HARPO (always the creeping id) necks a bottle of champagne, throws paper out of the waste bin and lights it with a flaming torch produced, suddenly, from his hat. He sits and warms his hands, and the fire, turned into something friendly, is impracticable.

> WILDE
> I'm glad to hear you smoke. A man
> should always have an occupation of
> some kind.

The Marx Bros. think again.

When they wanted to stay in the hotel, one of them had to pretend to be ill. Now that they want to leave the hotel, one of them has to pretend to be dead. Leo, they decide, must pretend to kill himself.

> CHICO
> He drinks a bottle of poison. We have
> to rush him to the hospital. They'll
> have to let us through.

(Dora mentions suicide in a letter. She puts it away in a drawer; her father finds it nonetheless.)

The Marx Bros. put Leo into the bed in the bridal suite. It is a single bed, pink and chintzy. Leo's LOVE INTEREST enters. She should be anguished, but she is undramatic, or perhaps she's no actress.

> LOVE INTEREST
> (flatly)
> Mr Gribble said you were dying.

(Dora saw Herr K walking down the street. He was knocked over by a car. She didn't show immediate distress; she didn't stick around to see what happened.)

                    LEO
              (who is a playwright)
          It's only a plot darling.

(That might have been parapraxis I mean a joke.)

                    LEO
              (pretends to be dead)

                    CHICO
          All he said was, "Mother!"

                    WILDE
          (in that comedy of the mystery of
          maternity, The Importance of Being
          Earnest)
          Mother!

               HOTEL INSPECTOR
          You struggle for money. What
          good is it. You never know who's
          next. . . . Too bad he didn't die
          at the Aster.

CHICO, GROUCHO (HARPO) sing "Swing Low, Sweet Chariot, Coming For To Carry Me Home" and take Leo out of the hotel and into the theater. The hotel's exit is around the back. It is small, an emergency exit, for things that should not be taken through the hotel entrance, which we never see. Leaving the hotel is more difficult than it seems.

They arrive in the theater or, rather, they are already there. We don't see how they get in, but they had no need to leave the hotel. Leo's play takes place (as in a dream) in a theater that appears on the premises. The play that is staged in the luxury hotel is about miners. The actors enter carrying shovels, to show their trade.

                        WILDE
    I am glad to say that I have never
    seen a spade!

The play appears to be a serious play, a play about social issues, about hard work, and also about death (it is a tragedy); it is about things that cannot be given house room in the hotel. The play takes place in the country. There are no hotels there. It is a play about people who cannot afford to stay in hotels, or to go to the theater. When the actors call each other "comrade," everyone applauds (it is 1938).

Hidden in the audience, Leo gives himself away by calling "Author! Author!" He calls for himself in the third person, as he is dead. HARPO appears on stage playing dead, on a bier. Though his appearance must have been unexpected, none of the actors seems surprised. Harpo wears a lumberjack shirt, which fits the action of the play. No one is sad. This is because he is only acting. But the actors have stopped acting (if they were still acting, they'd act sad). Or maybe the play has changed from a tragedy to a comedy.

Death, like Wilde's hotel, is beyond my means. A hotel is nowhere to end up, not really. Tragedy is impossible there. Death in a hotel—what a joke! Wilde was right. In a hotel, death is deflected as it is by a joke, where meaning is never allowed to dwell for long. It blocks any hope of ending. But I might like to die in a hotel, clinically, on clean sheets, to make a clean sweep onto a tabula rasa, like being born. Famous last words?

ALL
(singing, onstage and off)
Swing low, sweet chariot, coming for to carry me home.

8 THE TALKING CURE

"The capacity of lacerating accusation to indwell may be such that while its target is fearful that it may be true, she's also fearful that it may not be true, which would force the abandonment of her whole story."
—DENISE RILEY, *LANGUAGE AS AFFECT*

```
Cast:
Freud:            a psychoanalyst
Dora:             a teenage girl
KM:               a guest
```

I

So I wrote my hotel reviews, and I was not paid, but I exchanged words for things, the sort of things you find in hotels. The exchange rate was not set, but the exchange always happened. My words enacted off the page, and some kind of transference occurred, or rather, my words pre-acted, as I often knew what was required of my writing before I'd stayed. It was a matter of formula. My words were turned into white beds, and white baths, and towelling robes, and dinners, none of which I could hold onto, none of which I wanted to. In the end the things were more transient than the words, in that they stopped, and the words are still there.

Katherine Mansfield wrote a story in which the daughter of Baroness von Gall came to the German Pension to take the cure. She was dumb. She was there, perhaps, for a talking cure. The guests could not tell, because the baroness's daughter could not tell them. She also could not tell them that her companion, whom they so fêted, was not the baroness's unwed sister, but her maid.

Aphonia is only interesting in the unmarried. So is talking.

KM

```
Love which becomes engaged and married
is a purely affirmative affair.
```

I have been (or possibly am still) married and I claim the right to words. But what can I say? I can tell and tell and talking does not change anything, not even in me.

I am in my hotel, and you are not there. I thought the hotel would be an escape from you but instead your absence fills it, though, in the hotel, there is nothing of you. I don't want to talk to you anyway. I can't get on with you. I can't get on without talking to you. If we talk to each other we will say nothing. You like to talk to me about things, about *things* I mean, like beds, and baths, and towelling robes, and dinners. You like to talk to me only if nothing is said.

The screen fills the screen, waiting for the talking to begin. (The talking that is, of course, writing.)

It does not, so it is never disappointing.

I only want to talk to you when I am not talking to you.

And then I want to talk to you all the time.

You can say "My love," and do nothing loving. Whenever you say it, I believe it.

It is a word without symptoms, unless you count those in me.

I am your word's symptom.

Dora's aphonia, said Freud, was a "conversion disorder" of mental into physical symptoms. The exchange rate was not set, but the conversion always happened. Aphonia is only one possible hysterical symptom, but it is not the complaint. Hysteria is the complaint.

Some women go to hotels in order to complain.

Some women go to hotels for a cure.

Others go for the talking cure.

Freud talked to Dora, then he talked about Dora (to herself), then he wrote about Dora. Through it all she continued to complain with her silent body, which could have meant anything. We don't even see her. We can only read his words. Show the body; take the body away. Distance is the only cure. Getting away is a question not only of space, but time. And aphonia makes sense to me, even now.

FREUD

She had been listening, without
contradicting as she usually did. She
seemed moved, said goodbye as sweetly
as anything, with warmest wishes for
the new year and—never came back.

Freud will not call Dora back.	(You will not call me back.)
Dora will not demand a cure.	(I will not demand a cure.)
They will use no more words on each other.	(We will use no more words.)

Aphonia. If you won't talk to me, at least I can write it down.

FREUD

She lived for her studies, and did not
think of marriage.

In the end, Dora cured herself by talking, but not to Freud. She told Frau K she knew of her father's affair. She "forced" (says Freud) Herr K to admit "the scene by the lake." (It *was* a scene, like in a play, just as Freud told her: those canvas trees, those references to high art, that turned into sex.)

Herr K admitted Dora was right.

One need only turn each individual
reproach back on the speaker.

The right words had been there all the time.

Dora had only to wait for the right speaker.

II

On the screen, I keep checking the time: where I am, where you are, the thickness of hours between.

I cannot wait any longer.

The thick white hotel towels are restless. They want me to get into the water. There are the white pills. Usually you snap them in half, which makes a satisfactory sound—no, the echo of a sound, no noise.

My head put the noise in.

I cannot remember the time where you are. It's in a different zone. I look. Then away, then back again. I still cannot remember.

What's the right time? I can wait a little longer before we speak.

Whatever time it is you will not answer, not with anything I can hear.

There is no point looking up the time any more.

And then I know the time. But it's no use. Whatever time it is where you are, what I say will disappoint you in the end.

White invites a sacrifice.

The square white bath has a crack across its corner. I turn on the tap. I get into the bath. It bends and bows. It circles the square. A pool pools underneath. I call room service. It is not my fault, but I must leave the room and walk through the white streets under the white sun until it is fixed.

It is *not* my fault.

The thing is: What am I allowed? If I don't *need* anything in particular, what am I allowed to want? What should I do with this blank hotel opportunity for which I've worked so hard? Can I only see myself in what I want, and can I only want something when something else goes wrong?

When you're not here, sometimes the problem doesn't seem to be you. It doesn't seem to be you at all.

Perhaps this is only ordinary unhappiness.

9 HOTEL MARX

"To put it metaphorically: it is entirely possible that a diurnal thought should act as the entrepreneur for the dream; but the entrepreneur, who, as they say, has the idea and the drive to put it into action, can do nothing without capital; he requires a capitalist with the necessary outlay, and that capitalist, who provides the psychical outlay . . . is a desire from the unconscious."
—SIGMUND FREUD, *DORA: A FRAGMENT*

```
Cast:
Freud:                    a psychoanalyst
Dora:                     a teenage girl
Kringelein:               a clerk
Gruskinskaya (Garbo):     a star
Raoul Vaneigem:           a philosopher
```

I

I went to my doctor, and described my symptoms.

My doctor said, "You're not depressed, you're oppressed."

But then, she was not a therapist.

We used to watch old movies together, you and I. It was one of the things we didn't fail to do. When there was something wrong with what was in front of us, which was surely not the same as what was real, we watched movies. That they were old movies helped: anything over was better than anything current. They were always on repeat, and always free. We could watch them over and over again, catching them at non-times, in the middle of white afternoons. As we withdrew further into the movies, the more we leant toward the things in them, until we could recognize ourselves in them, or thought we could. We watched movies from the era when, and the places where, people lived in hotels, and many of the movies were about hotels, more than were about homes. A hotel is easy to recreate on a sound stage, because it looks just like a set. A hotel is a dream and must avoid the disappointments of the actual, but it requires something physical: an entrepreneur to provide the furniture for desire. And it is made of both human and inhuman materials.

An evening alone in hotel world: On the inedible room service menu, a list of hermetically sealed in-hotel channels. I look for something that will square both our moods: the hotel's and mine. The biggest category is "fantasy and adventure," candy-colored: nothing I do here will matter. There are also video games; this hotel's less for playboys than for boys who like to play. I look for a hotel movie. When I type "hotel" I don't know what language I'll get: hotel is the same word round the globe. I find *Grand Hotel* (Goulding 1932). I've seen it before. Its black and white matches my room's theme but the Grand Hotel doesn't remind me of any hotel I have visited. In the opening centrifugal spin around its circular reception desk, shot from above, more guests come and go than in the lonely lobbies where I have lingered. To make himself heard, dying clerk Kringelein (Lionel Barrymore) must shout into the lobby's public telephone about the most private things: "HE SAYS I WON'T LIVE MUCH LONGER!" You'd imagine the hotel bar and ballroom were the most popular spots in town, yet Greta Garbo went there "to be alone."

"A private room with a bath!" demands Kringelein, who has come to the Grand Hotel to spend his last pennies. He demands a more impressive room, and finds exclusivity is the long climb to the loneliness of the fifth floor. Even there, privacy is always being invaded. Typist Flaemmchen (Joan Crawford) catches her employer Preysling (Wallace Beery) in his bath, and jewel thief/Baron (John Barrymore) climbs from balcony to balcony, peering through each window in search of an easy mark. *I want to be alone!*

Privacy is the Grand Hotel's most expensive luxury, but to be served is to be known. In her suite, Grusinskaya's (Garbo) gowns spill out of her cases. You can see everything, but there's nothing to get a grip on. The eye slips off furnishings of blurred satin. Everything is white: her dresses, her sheets, her delightful body, her pearls, but she is the only character that is never alone. Watched by her maid even when asleep, she exists only in front of an audience. There is no privacy in the Grand Hotel.

The movie's a "portmanteau" piece: a suitcaseful of stories, interrelated but distinct. And they are stories of disconnected people. None of the people in *Grand Hotel* are married, or, if they are, their wives, their husbands are absent, or they are escaping them, just like in the German Pension. Perhaps there are no stories to tell about marriage, or they are too difficult to tell. Family is a private matter, kept at home behind closed doors like a case of syphilis, a case of hysteria. Disconnection is a hotel tragedy, but also its opportunity. None of the guests understands anyone else's troubles: There are frequent mistakes—of identity, of meaning—that allow stories to happen, but they are stories like jokes: they deflect. Where there is no privacy, there is no possibility of connection.

Something about the entire movie fails to connect: so many stars, all playing a different style and genre. It's funny because it's a Hollywood film set in Berlin, but filmed on a California sound stage barely into the sound era. All the actors are speaking English, but some with fake (or real) European accents. Garbo plays a Swedish-accented Russian; Beery, playing a German, talks to Crawford, also playing a German, but his voice is mitteleuropa, whereas hers is pure USA.

And all the performances are different. Lionel Barrymore's a ham, but then he's playing one—a stage drunk, his silent-movie gestures too large for the screen—it's impossible to draw a line between the performance and the part. Joan Crawford, who was never a silent star like Garbo, is subtle, physically contained, wordy. John Barrymore (the Baron) is a blank-faced matinee idol, but Wallace Beery (Preysling) is understated, naturalistic, though he's playing a bumptious bore. Garbo, playing dancer Grusinskya, doesn't look much like a ballerina and she's never seen dancing, but it doesn't matter a bit. On stage, we're told, she's a "natural," but she can only wow the audience when inspired by the "real thing": love. She's unaware that, offstage, she's pure performance.

```
                    GRUSINSKAYA
     I can't dance tonight.
```

But she does. She always does.

"You're entirely different from what I expected," says Presyling when he finds Flaemmchen's performance as a sex object is just as formal as her performance as a typist. Flaemmchen, the ambiguous stenographer who also poses for "art studies," is the butt of the film's sexual jokes and double meanings. She's constantly mistaken for a prostitute, and no wonder: she's always telling us what she's worth ("I got ten Marks for it," she says of her magazine centerfold). From the same social class as Kringelein, they are both earners of "little pennies." Everyone needs so many of these pennies to pay the hotel bill but, while they gain it, they must pretend not to be working. The leisure industry's a factory floor. What does a hotel cost per minute? When you get the bill it's the extras that bring you down. Sometimes it's breakfast; sometimes it's the WiFi. Sometimes it's things you don't even know you're enjoying.

> KRINGELEIN
> (On the lobby telephone)
> Every minute costs 2 marks 90. . . . I want to explain, but I must do so quickly, it costs so much.

Does Flaemmchen enjoy her typist day job? It seems not. Does she even enjoy the perks of her "hotel" job that come from closer acquaintance with her employers? Not as much as we might have hoped. But she has to look as if she does, in order to procure them—service *and* a smile: that's the hotel industry. Flaemmchen's ambiguity, which insists that any pretty girl can be bought for a night like a suite, is at the heart of the hotel's glamour, even if it refuses to acknowledge she's on the unofficial payroll. Like all the characters, she has to pretend not to be what she is not, but to be what she is.

Only Flaemchenn, who understands this play of surfaces better than most, can convert them into an act of generosity. "Dance with old Kringelein," says the Baron. And she does, smiling, though the Baron knows she really wants to dance with him. What cruelty! How easily he acknowledges her hotel role. And Flaemmchen from that moment, recognizes herself as she is seen, just as Freud does in the mirror in the train bathroom. Accepting herself at face value, her hotel value (as Freud, outside his consulting room, appeared to himself as merely an old man), she goes upstairs to take up Preysling's offer of a trip to glamorous Manchester. At that instant she becomes like hotel staff—doomed to hanging around in corridors, in lobbies—but her position remains ambiguous; she's still not servant class

"Who are you really?" Garbo asks Baron Barrymore. No need to ask; we already know. *Grand Hotel* is a big-name picture, each actor performing what she, or he, does best. "There's no 'real thing,'" insists Crawford/Flaemmchen, only half joking, when Baron Barrymore rejects her for Garbo. Or so she must pretend, as her life (or her living) depends on it.

"I'm going to live!" boasts dying Kringelein, unaware that at the Grand Hotel, living is the last thing he'll do. Living at a hotel is hard work. Leisure, which is not the opposite but the corresponding state to work, is a tough job, and no movie mentions work so much. Clerk Kringelein knows the price of everything, and isn't afraid to point it out. This goes with a kind of naive impropriety. When he asks Flaemmchen, "Would you like to see my bathroom?," he is not being indecent; he's merely impressed by its size, and style.

Everyone is a workaholic nowadays, even when they're on holiday. Something's got to give.

I have never lived in a hotel. It has always been work.

II

One cannot now live in a hotel—the economics are impossible. Once upon a time people did, though seldom in hotels like the *Grand Hotel*. They were women mostly, women without men: Katherine Mansfield's heroines, and also her villains, their husbands elsewhere, for her villains were often married. Those were hotels for single women, in single rooms, for maids, and old maids, like Charlotte Bartlett in E. M. Forster's *A Room with a View* (she scarcely exists in the novel out of them). Hotels were the only place these women were served, had anyone to serve them. They were the only place they existed in public.

Nowadays hotels are for couples, a brief escape from their family selves, and, for single people, mostly only if they are on business, though they will be charged for the empty half of their double beds (perhaps some are paying for the opportunity to fill that space). Hotels are also the places couples look most uncomfortable. They go to hotels to discover their differences. They are altered, in this public space where, suddenly, they must both perform their value, and they sometimes discover that one of them has more value, though the woman must always wear her value on her sleeve. The man's value is more often hidden, but may be guessed at, partly by looking at the woman he is with.

Sometimes you went to hotels for business. The hotels you went to were called business hotels, though you only spent your leisure time in them, and did your business elsewhere. The hotels I went to for work were called hotels for leisure. As a hotel reviewer, I sometimes took you to leisure hotels, but the fit was never right. What sort of marriage were we performing there?

In leisure hotels, you had to perform being a man, being part of a couple. As you didn't enjoy this performance, hotel visits were seldom enjoyable, on my face across the table that expression I saw mirrored in yours, like chewing something you can't get out of your teeth: a nothing-to-be-done face.

"How are you?" I said. You said:

"Sad, as I always am in transition."

It is the only place I am happy.

All the things we hardly dared to do together.

III

I'm back in the *vorhof*, the vestibule, the only place, in *Grand Hotel* the movie, where we see the hotel staff.

```
                VANEIGEM
The bourgeois no-man's-land of
exchange.
```

I have my copy of *The Revolution of Everyday Life* by Raoul Vaneigem.

The lobby is where the exchange goes on, furtive. I am leaving the hotel (to go, where?). I don't pay, also furtively; I don't want the others to know I'm getting it all, apparently, for free.

(I enclose myself in embarrassing parentheses.)

VANEIGEM
Nothing moving, only dead time
passing.

In a hotel, as in a hospital, I am not at home. I am required to do no home work. Ordinary things are done for me: cooking, shining shoes. I am rendered helpless. I have rendered myself helpless. I treat myself as I normally do others. It is, I suppose, a kind of self-othering. In a hotel I can get anything, anytime, but nothing I want, or need. It is a place where I am taught to become someone with desires, that is, someone whose desires meet what the hotel provides, on hotel terms—a hotel person. I've finally become someone, but I don't recognize myself. Like Freud in his railway carriage, here I am one side of the mirror, and, (equally, but differently) on the other: "Hello." In a hotel, I'm always searching for the reflexive verb. Could it be self-serving?

This desire to serve—is it selfless, or selfish? There are hotels where you can self-serve—a credit card in the door, you'll never see anyone lower down the order than yourself. Now that's a real isolation unit. It's not for me. In a hotel, whether guest or staff, I relax in the presence of someone else's authority. But what about the flipside: the servers (now that's the name for an implement)? Service is a strong word. Things can be put into it, and taken out of it again. Something can be made to serve, as can someone, for the time being, in a hotel as it can at home, though it's easier here; in a hotel at least you can get rid of your server with a tip, however awkward the tipping point.

It's surprising how few of the stories in *Grand Hotel* concern the staff—apart from frontman Senff (Jean Hersholt), the servers are content to remain ghosts. Senff is an unsatisfactory character who seldom steps beyond the lobby, either into or out of the hotel. He remains at reception by the switchboard, which is as much of a character as he is, in this movie about switched connections. Only once, in the film's opening scene, does Senff the ghost porter overstep a boundary, using a hotel line to call the hospital about his pregnant wife. Life happens (people are born) outside the hotel, especially for Senff, whose story never crosses any of the other strands of plot. His connections with the guests are purely professional and he is necessarily fooled by appearances; it's part of his job. "I don't believe it!" is his response to the revelation that the Baron is a thief. "I know people."

Do I know what serves me, and is it the same thing I am serving?

What do the waiters look like when they take off their waistcoats, those black waistcoats with the multiple pockets like ticket pockets but longer, slanted horizontal? Do they look like stripped penguins? The pockets are laid flat against their abdomens. In them, they keep different denominations, but you cannot see the shape of what they will bring out, only that there are little slits in their sides, ranked like ribs, out of which and into which they can put surprising things. Permeability is a feature of abjection. It is the human made serviceable. The abject is what a hospital cannot treat, and maybe not even a clinic. Despite its holes, it insists on still existing. It keeps on going, just as though it were a person: self-serving, unpermeated, whole. The abject is also what we need to remain abject, what we desire to continue to exist to serve us; what we need to expel, pay off, need not to acknowledge as quite human—dress it up in what uniform you like.

Abjection literally means "the state of being cast off."

Dora gave Freud fourteen days' notice of quitting.

She paid Freud for his services, but it was she who gave notice.

> FREUD
> That sounds like a serving girl, or a governess.

But Freud did not say who, in this scenario, was the server, who was the served.

Dora cast off Freud, in the end. She cast off everyone: her family, their friends. She went away to stay, perhaps, at a hotel, where she was clean, clean as a hotel bathroom. *She lived for her studies, and did not think of marriage.* She was no longer dirty, was not put to use. She was no longer abject, at the mercy. . . . Maybe it was lonely. Maybe things couldn't enact, not even words, after she refused to employ any actors. Eventually, said Freud, "life would win her back." When life won, we hear no more from Dora. Did she lose, perhaps?

I can leave. No one's stopping me. That's the difficult thing. No one's stopping me from doing anything. But it's so difficult to lack all obstacles.

I must learn to live without the hope of serving, of being served.

I must learn to live without hope.

(This is not as hopeless as it sounds.)

IV

At the end of *Grand Hotel*, the Doctor (Lewis Stone), who is not the hotel dick, but, as in *Room Service*, acts as a kind of moral policeman, insists that, in the hotel, "nothing ever happens," but the old cynic is barking up the wrong tree. We're meant immediately to notice he's wrong, as the movie's full of action—but the illusion is that it ever comes to anything.

Grand Hotel is a movie about illusion, pretense, imitation, including the illusion that its stories have endings. It starts with endings: clerk Kringelein dying, Grusinskaya at the end of her career, Baron (John) Barrymore on his uppers, Beery Preysling demanding more drink to down the dregs of his failing company. "This is the end," says Garbo/Grusinskaya, "I always said I'd leave off when the time came." But she doesn't; at the Grand Hotel no one can. Everyone goes on and on repeating just what they did before. Grusinskaya returns to dancing; Preysling hangs onto his company with a lie; Kringelein, despite his decline, spins out through the hotel's plate glass revolving door—a style that has migrated from hotels and is now more likely to be found in offices— in the movie's final shot, Flaemmchen on his arm, with all appearance of gusto, forgetting the Baron's death in his determination to perform for the next Grand Hotel.

Maybe Kringelein found a cure. It looks like he was never ill.

10 POSTCARDS FROM 26 HOTELS

"Guess Rome was where we saw the yellow dog."
E. M. FORSTER, *A ROOM WITH A VIEW*

Hotel A

In a niche set on the stairs between each floor, an artwork representing a woman who was alive once, in the style of artists who also lived, but not painted by these artists, and not painted in the presence of the woman, who died some centuries ago.

Hotel B

In the lift shaft: stencils of skeletal figures by an artist who usually graffitis the outside of buildings.

Hotel C

The ceiling in the restaurant, painted with blackboard paint. Words on it. The chicken: too salty.

Hotel D

A president and a famous movie director have stayed here, among others. I bled on the sheets, unexpectedly, washed them in the shower, and dried them with the electric hairdryer. The mushrooms were salty.

Hotel E

It makes me shy to eat such a grand dinner in the empty restaurant at lunchtime. It makes me shy to swim alone in the circular basement pool.

Hotel F

The basement restaurant where we were served a scotch egg: the smart kind, and perfectly done, but . . .

Hotel G

On Easter Day they gave us hard-boiled eggs dipped in red or blue paint, at breakfast.

Hotel H

Where there was a rainstorm, and I was tired, so I called up room service, who came with a trolley and on it some slices of the kind of cheese with a straw in the middle.

Hotel I

I was frightened to go to the (excellent) nightly dinner because the waiter did not like that I could not finish the homemade pasta.

Hotel J

I remember the graffiti outside the hotel, but nothing of the hotel.

Hotel K

My deluxe room was "orange."

Hotel L

I don't remember staying here at all. Maybe another reviewer covered it. The style in which the hotel is reviewed is, however, indistinguishable from mine.

Hotel M

The skirting board was chipped. While having sex, I noted that, as the hotel manager had told me, I could see the Eiffel Tower in the distance through the window.

Hotel N

The lift shaft rumbled all night. I put my laptop on the windowsill for WiFi. The room was small and unsatisfactory. The steak tartare was good, but not included in the price.

Hotel O

It was expensive, but truly horrible.

Hotel P

The bathwater wouldn't run warm. I was so tired I could neither understand, nor complain.

Hotel Q

Here I also became ill. Unsure as to whether I would have to pay extra, I skipped the breakfast buffet to go to a cafe with a friend.

Hotel R

In this hotel a friend's husband got me drunk and tried to sleep with me. That was in older days, (or do I mean younger?) when I was hardly able to recognize what he was trying to do.

Hotel S

It was so hot outside and so cold inside. Elvis Presley played in the lift. The same song, every time.

Hotel T

When I arrived, they brought me tea in a Chinese padded basket, and little cakes. I have never been so grateful for anything.

Hotel U

Was brown. I couldn't close the skylight. The noise from the club across the road kept me awake all night.

Hotel V

The room was on the sixth floor, an attic. The instructions in case of fire were no more than hopeful.

Hotel W

Was grand, but very ugly. And reception was on the second floor.

Hotel X

In the lounge, they had copper doors with bullet holes from a revolution.

Hotel Y

I got drunk in this hotel, as in several others.

Hotel Z

It was above a pub. I ate raw meat, and cooked potatoes. I am tired of hotels now.

NOTES

Chapter 1

1 Kierkegaard, Søren, *Repetition and Philosophical Crumbs*, trans. Piety (Oxford, UK: Oxford University Press, 2009), 5.

All Vaneigem quotes from: Vaneigem, Raoul, *The Revolution of Everyday Life*, trans. Donald Nicholson-Smith (Norfolk, UK: Rebel Press, 2006), 30.

Chapter 2

1 *The Register News* (Mt. Vernon, IL), October 25, 1949.

2 It isn't.

All Janet Malcolm quotes from: Janet Malcolm, *The Impossible Profession* (London, UK: Picador, 1988).

All Freud quotes from: Sigmund Freud, *Psychology of Love* (London, UK: Penguin, 2006), unless otherwise stated.

Chapter 3

1 Sigmund Freud, *The Penguin Freud Reader* (London, UK: Penguin, 2006), 462.

Chapter 4

1 Sigmund Freud, *Complete Works*, trans. Strachey, vol. 7 (London, UK: Vintage, 1905).

2 http://www.etymonline.com/index.php?term=dwell.

3 Homer, *Odyssey*, Book 19, trans. A. T. Murray (Cambridge, MA: Harvard University Press, 1919).

All Heidegger quotes from: Martin Heidegger, *Building Dwelling Thinking, in Poetry, Language, Thought* (London, UK: HarperCollins, 1971).

Chapter 5

1 Michel Foucault, *Birth of The Clinic* (London, UK: Routledge, 2003), 4.

2 Although this quote is widespread online, I can find no confirmed source. It is possibly fictional.

3 Sigmund Freud, *The Interpretation of Dreams, Complete Works*, trans. Strachey, vol. 4 (London, UK: Vintage, 1955), 844.

4 Sigmund Freud, Dora, cited in introduction by Phillip Rieff (New York, USA: Touchstone Books, 1977), vii.

5 Sigmund Freud, *The Uncanny, Complete Works*, trans. Strachey, vol. 17 (London, UK: Vintage, 1955), 248.

Chapter 6

1 Simon Louvish, *Mae West: It Ain't No Sin* (New York: Macmillan, 2006), 350–51.

2 Another untraceable Mae West quote.

3 http://thestir.cafemom.com/pregnancy/162567/every_
   woman_deserves_a_swanky.

4 http://www.mommyish.com/2013/10/13/couple-gives-birth-
   in-hotel-room/.

5 Sigmund Freud, "A Case of Hysteria", *Complete Works*,
   trans. Strachey, vol. 7 (London, UK: Vintage, 1955), 90.

6 Sigmund Freud, *Inhibitions, Symptoms and Anxiety*, *Complete
   Works*, trans. Strachey, vol. 20 (London, UK: Vintage,
   1959), 91.

7 Sigmund Freud, *The Interpretation of Dreams*, *Complete
   Works*, trans. Strachey, vol. 5 (London, UK: Vintage, 1955), 17.

8 Sigmund Freud, letter, cited in Eran J. Rolnik, *Freud in Zion:
   Psychoanalysis and the Making of Modern Jewish Identity*
   (London: Karnac Books, 2012), 141.

9 Denise Riley, *Impersonal Passion, Language as Affect* (Durham,
   NC: Duke University Press, 2005), 51.

   All Katherine Mansfield quotes from: *Katherine Mansfield),
   Collected* Stories (London, UK: Penguin, 1981). All Oscar
   Wilde quotes from: Oscar Wilde, *The Importance of Being
   Earnest* (London: Methuen, 1981).

Chapter 7

1 https://www.nuh.nhs.uk/patients-and-visitors/hospital-hotel/.

2 None of these Wilde quotations can be verified.

3 Charlotte Chandler, *Hello, I Must Be Going: Groucho and His Friends* (London: Sphere Books, 1987). All Oscar Wilde quotes from: Oscar Wilde, *The Importance of Being Earnest* (London: Methuen, 1981).

All *Room Service* quotes from my transcript of the movie.

Chapter 9

All *Grand Hotel* quotes from my transcription of the movie.

ACKNOWLEDGMENTS

Thank you, early readers Isabella Streffen, Tristram Burke, John Toby Ferris, Richard Barnett, and Sharon Kivland, and my first reader, as always, Lauren Elkin. Thank you, Deborah Levy, for guiding me to the German Pension. Thank you again, Deborah, and also Brian Dillon, and Olivia Laing, for sponsoring my proposal.

INDEX